REMATCH
Winning Legal Battles
With Your Ex

Steven R. Lake
with Ruth Duskin Feldman

CHICAGO REVIEW PRESS

Printed in the United States of America
First Edition
1 2 3 4 5 6 7 8 9 10

Published by Chicago Review Press, Incorporated,
814 North Franklin Street, Chicago, Illinois, 60610

ISBN 1-55652-053-0

For J. R.

CONTENTS

AUTHOR'S NOTE

As I said in *Hearts and Dollars,* I am not a do-it-yourself advocate. I write books for lay people so that they *don't* do it themselves and can recognize when they may need professional help.

Laws are constantly changing. Any attempt to tell you what the law is on a particular topic could be wrong before the ink is dry.

The case histories in this book are based on facts, but the names and occupations of the parties have been changed to protect their confidentiality. In a few cases we have used actual names; however, these have been previously published and are already a matter of public record.

ACKNOWLEDGMENTS

Although two names appear on the cover of this book, a third deserves equal billing—my sister, Andrea Gold. Andrea earned a degree in education from the University of Illinois in 1973 and taught elementary school for a few years until the birth of her first child.

Now the mother of three, Andrea balances an active life as a wife and homemaker with her new profession as a paralegal.

When my office staff collectively grimaced at my announcement that I was going to write another book, I asked Andrea if she would assist me with the research for *Rematch*.

Not having worked on a project with Andrea since I had helped her with her geometry homework, I didn't know what to expect; but her talent proved beyond my best expectations.

It was no easy task gathering the statistical information contained in the following pages. Andrea was thorough, persistent, and resourceful, and she deserves a great deal of credit. She is truly a pro.

I would also like to thank Ruth Duskin Feldman. Ruth is a journalist and author or coauthor of four other books and numerous newspaper and magazine articles. She did an excellent job of combining my ideas, anecdotes, and observations with the raw data provided in the research. I believe the result is a very readable text dealing with some complex social and legal issues.

Finally, although my office staff grimaced, they did chip in. A special thanks goes to my partner, Alan Toback; attorneys Julie Parker and Judy Brenner; accountants Michael Heneghan and Stuart Levin; my secretary Beth Forgette; and my good friend, Sandy Siepak.

INTRODUCTION: THE BATTLE OF THE "EXES"

Marriage in America has become a revolving door. Forty percent of all marriages in the United States—more than 1.2 million each year—end in dissolution and disillusion. Nearly 14 million Americans are divorced, and that doesn't include the one-third of all currently-marrieds whose previous unions failed. Among women now in their late thirties, the figures are even more startling. Projections are that 56 percent of these "baby boomers" will go through divorce sooner or later, and of the 70 percent who remarry, more than half will be divorced again.

Any of these people—perhaps you—are potential candidates for a rematch: a return bout in the arena of the legal system. Easily half of my practice as a Chicago divorce lawyer concerns legal conflicts and actions that arise after a marriage is officially dead.

In addition, changing lifestyles and the resulting increase in cohabitation have produced a different kind of uncoupling: the split-up of unwed partners. An estimated 2.6 million unmarried, unrelated couples—representing one out of 35 American households—now live together. Here, too, the end of a relationship can be just the start of a series of legal maneuvers.

Much of the continuing tension between ex-mates or ex-lovers grows out of their mutual roles as parents. Nearly 15 million children in the United States—about 1 in 4—live with a single parent, 90 percent of them with the mother. Nearly two-thirds of these youngsters have parents who are divorced or separated; more than one-fourth were born out of wedlock. And the trend is growing: estimates are that up to half of all children born today will be raised by a single parent.

Children are often the biggest losers in the "battle of the exes." Disputes over child support, custody, and visitation—even charges of child abuse and parental kidnapping—are increasingly common. Grandparents, brothers, sisters, and other family members, too, may be caught in the tug-of-war.

Why You Need This Book

You may be thinking that the subject of this book is rather specialized; that it applies only to people who have been divorced or who have broken up an unwed relationship. Actually, the scope is broader than that. If you're in the process of divorce, if you're only beginning to contemplate divorce, or if you're currently involved in a nonmatrimonial relationship, you need the information contained in these pages. This book will explain what can happen to you and those who intimately touch your life—your children, your parents, new spouses, and new lovers—after a marital or nonmarital breakup.

If, for example, your ex is harassing you, refusing to pay alimony or child support or to let you see the children, neglecting or abusing them, or threatening to take them out of state, your hands are not tied. There's much you can do to protect yourself and your family if you're aware of your rights and remedies. If your ex tries to haul you into court with a claim of nonsupport or denial of visitation rights, you need to know what your obligations are and how to avoid unnecessary trouble. If you have joint custody and it's not working, you need to know what you can do about it. In these and many other situations that arise, you need to know what you can do on your own, how to refrain from actions that may jeopardize your interests, when to call upon legal counsel, what questions to ask, and how to tell whether you're getting the advice and assistance you need.

Divorce Isn't the Last Word

Divorce is far from the last word when spouses split up. Because divorce courts have broad discretion to enforce, change, or revoke previous orders, it's important to be alert to the legal possibilities and pitfalls after a divorce.

Decrees, orders, and agreements don't magically enforce themselves. You need to make sure your ex-spouse lives up to his or her end of the arrangement. Furthermore, the terms can sometimes be changed; or the decree itself, under certain circumstances, can be thrown out.

Many people don't realize that they may be able to alter an unsatisfactory agreement. They just assume it's a lost cause. On the other hand, some are overly complacent. They got what was coming to them, or so they think—not realizing that a disgruntled ex, with the help of a clever lawyer, may find a way to turn the tables.

If, at this point, you're only considering divorce, you need to look ahead so as to avoid hasty, ill-considered actions or omissions that could jeopardize your interests afterwards. If you're headed for your second or third divorce, you may need advice to avoid the mistakes you made the last time.

This book will help you to foresee and handle issues that could result in post-divorce lawsuits and will show you what to do if you're faced with legal action or if you wish to initiate it. I'll point out how laws and judicial precedents vary from one state to another, and some of the ways in which they have changed and are changing.

Ending an Unwed Relationship May Not Be Simple

Many people who break off live-in or casual relationships think they're home free. There was no marital contract, so it's easy to kiss and say goodbye. Right?

Wrong. As I pointed out in *Hearts and Dollars: How to Beat the High Cost of Falling In and Out of Love*, living with a lover of either sex can be a legal time bomb. And I'm not just talking about "palimony" cases, like the sensational ones involving Lee Marvin, Hugh Hefner, Liberace, and Billie Jean King.

What if, several years down the road, an illegitimate child suddenly appears (as happened to Hefner), claiming support or inheritance rights? New, reliable scientific paternity tests—along with the extension of time limits on filing paternity cases—make it much easier for a woman (or a man) to establish paternity and the resulting legal rights and obligations.

Some unmarried women decide that they want to become mothers without a marriage commitment. Such a woman may make a deal with a man: "Give me a couple thousand dollars for medical expenses, and you'll never hear from me again." Later the man may be hit with an unexpected lawsuit for child support. On the other side of the coin, the father may decide he wants to see his child and may get a court order for visitation, when the woman wants nothing further to do with him.

Holding Your Ex-Sex Partner Accountable

What can you do if your husband, wife, or lover gave you AIDS or herpes, forced you to have an abortion, or caused you to become impotent or sterile? You can sue; and an increasing number of people are doing it. Such "sexual liability" cases, which seek to hold spouses and sex partners legally responsible for the results of their actions, present a new and growing area of jurisprudence, which I'll discuss in the last chapter.

An Overview

In the following chapters, I'll describe how you might become embroiled in a legal dispute with your ex, and I'll identify factors that may affect the outcome. I'll suggest some simple steps you can take to protect your rights and interests, your safety, and your peace of mind. I'll tell you how to protect the benefits you've won and how you might even get a better deal. I'll also explain how to prevent chronic, costly litigation and how to defend yourself if faced with it.

In part 1, I'll describe some of the circumstances that might lead you back to court with your ex. I'll introduce you to the basic principles that are involved in litigation following a divorce or the ending of an unwed relationship. And I'll tell you how to keep your ex from harassing you.

In part 2, I'll discuss how to get what's coming to you. I'll tell you how to protect your property settlement, how to make your ex pay the maintenance or child support the court ordered, and how to stop interference with your visitation rights.

In part 3, I'll explain what kinds of changes you may be able to make in your decree, order, or agreement, such as a change of custody or an increase or decrease in child support or alimony. I'll also point out some unusual circumstances that sometimes result in invalidating a decree or paternity finding.

In part 4, I'll explain how third parties—such as grandparents, siblings, new spouses, or new lovers—may become innocent victims. And I'll tell you what to do if your ex abuses or kidnaps your child.

Finally, in part 5, I'll touch on two important new developments: (1) recent changes in the tax code that can profoundly affect your divorce settlement, and (2) the trend toward allowing damage suits by spouses, ex-spouses, and sex partners.

The end of a relationship is rarely pleasant. Now you will learn what to do when the unpleasantness drags on.

PART I

Scrappily Ever After

1

SO YOU THOUGHT
YOUR DIVORCE WAS
FINAL?

No matter how painful the process of getting a divorce may be, most people feel tremendous relief when it's over. At last they can go on with their lives, or so they think. Yet, in all likelihood, those same couples will someday be back in court. In fact, your chances of becoming involved in legal battles with your ex are greater after you're divorced than before. In Cook County, Illinois, for example, an estimated two to three times as many post-divorce motions were filed in 1988 as there were divorces granted that year.

Why Is There So Much Legal
Conflict Between Ex-Mates?

The end of a marriage is the beginning of a new relationship: being ex-mates. This relationship develops from the intricate network of legal obligations you incur when you become divorced—obligations that one or both of you may at some point call upon the legal system to enforce, interpret, or change.

One obvious reason for the continuing conflict between ex-spouses has to do with the hostilities that cause a marriage to dissolve in the first place. A man and woman who had trouble working out disagreements when they were married generally find it no easier to do so after the marital link has been severed. Then, too, divorce itself is usually a highly emotional experience. The tensions are unlikely to just disappear the moment an agreement is signed or a decree entered.

While some couples do manage to get through a breakup with a modicum of civility, others seem bound and determined to live scrappily ever after. Nothing seems to give them more pleasure than to make each other miserable. Tom may be seething because Sarah threw him over for another man. Sarah may be enraged because she believes she got the short end of the property settlement. These two have fought each other every inch of the way; why would they stop now? The divorce is just another chapter in a long personal vendetta.

Maybe Sarah moves in with her boyfriend, and Tom starts calling her every day at work or late at night, or comes around and threatens her. Maybe she writes nasty notes to his landlord or his employer. Such harassment can be extremely irritating or even frightening, and Tom or Sarah may need the help of knowledgeable professionals to deal with it.

Often an ex-husband or ex-wife tries to obtain by indirect means what he or she didn't get in the settlement. Agreements reached hastily, under the intense emotional pressure of a divorce proceeding, may leave one party or both feeling shortchanged.

Here's a common situation: Elizabeth's ex, Bill, felt so guilty about walking out on her that he was willing not only to give her alimony but to make the mortgage payments on the house (which she was awarded in the property settlement). Now, two months later, with his bills mounting, he sees things in a different light. Gradually he begins falling behind on the mortgage payments and finally stops making them altogether.

Or the shoe may be on the other foot: under the settlement

agreement, Elizabeth is supposed to put the house up for sale and divide the proceeds, but she refuses to do it. Initially, she may have been so shaken by Bill's rejection of her that she was willing to sign her name to almost anything, just to have the nightmare end. Now that the reality of her situation has sunk in, anger and indignation have taken over: "He walked out on me, and I have to move out of my house?"

Such changes of heart are the stuff that lawsuits are made of.

A "Friendly" Divorce Can Turn Unfriendly

Even if a divorce was fairly amicable and the settlement was satisfactory to both sides, conflicts are likely to arise—especially where children are concerned. Two people who have chosen to dissolve the bond of matrimony find that their lives remain intertwined in a web of support payments and visitation rights. Sometimes an accumulation of small breaches or oversights builds into a power struggle.

Let's say John is laid off from work for a few weeks, and he tells Louise she'll have to wait a while for the support payment that's due. Louise is supposed to send him a copy of the children's report cards; she "forgets" to do it, and when he calls to remind her, harsh words are exchanged. On his next scheduled visitation day, he comes to pick up the children and finds no one home. The following week, she sends him a bill for $600 for little Johnny's braces, and John tells her to go fly a kite.

What has happened here is that both John and Louise have taken the law into their own hands. Neither is living up to the terms of their divorce. Each may feel perfectly justified in his or her actions; she's not doing this because he's not doing that, and vice versa. But, to put it bluntly, both of them are violating the law. And, chances are, both will need to see lawyers before long.

Many times couples think it will be easier and friendlier to ignore the legalities and just deal with each other. If Hank gets a new sales job that prevents him from seeing the kids on Saturdays, his agreed-upon visitation day, he and his ex may simply decide between themselves to switch his visitation to Sundays.

That may work out fine for a while. But what if she decides to take the kids to her mother's one Sunday? "Look," she may point out, "it says right here in the decree that Saturday is your visitation day. I can't help it if you can't make it that day." Hank would have been on much safer ground if he had gone back to a judge (not necessarily the same one who granted the divorce) for a change in his visitation rights, or if he and his ex had negotiated an out-of-court resettlement agreement with the help of a lawyer.

As a divorce lawyer, I see cases like these nearly every day. Little irritations may build for a long time until some event that may or may not be directly connected with the point at issue triggers a legal action.

Often the trigger is economic. The person paying child support or alimony (sometimes called maintenance) may suffer financial reverses due to the loss of a job or a drop in the stock market. Inflation may alter one party's financial needs or the other party's ability to pay. One party may get an unexpected promotion or windfall. And a settlement that was reached under different conditions may now look disadvantageous or downright unfair.

A New Relationship Can Touch Off Legal Action

Another frequent trigger of litigation is a new relationship— marital or nonmarital—that replaces the old one.

Remarriage, which occurs within a year after the divorce in an estimated one out of five cases and eventually in nearly three out of four, usually brings financial adjustments to a divorce agreement. With another breadwinner in the picture, maintenance payments may be automatically terminated, and child support may have to be recalculated or renegotiated. Even if there's no provision for an automatic adjustment, the person making the payments (usually the man) may resent "paying through the nose" after his ex has remarried and may hire a lawyer to try to get him off the hook.

Many divorce decrees were entered at a time when the general practice was that alimony would end if the wife remarried. Nothing was said about cohabitation, however. Now most states have amended their laws so that living with someone on a continuing conjugal basis is considered the same as remarriage as far as terminating alimony is concerned.

Remarriage or a new nonmarital liaison may prompt a custody or visitation dispute. The children may not be happy with the new adult in the house and may decide they want to live with the other parent. A father may claim (rightly or wrongly) that his ex's new husband or lover is abusing the children or disciplining them too harshly, or that he has alcohol or drug problems. A mother may object to the children's being exposed to the influence of the father's new roommate.

A new relationship can have subtle psychological repercussions for the former mates, who may find themselves fighting about issues that weren't issues before. For example, a noncustodial father may fear that the mother's remarriage will result in his not being able to see his children. (Indeed, a survey of a nationally representative sample of 15,000 children found that, for whatever reasons, nearly half of those living with a remarried mother never see the father.)

One woman told me, "My ex has hardly bothered to see the kids in five years. All of a sudden, now, he says he wants joint custody."

"Have you remarried recently?" I asked her. I wasn't a bit surprised when she said yes.

In another case, a man I'll call Larry came to me complaining that his ex-wife, Donna, wasn't allowing him overnight visitations with his son on Saturdays, as provided in their decree. So, I filed a petition with the court. What Larry hadn't mentioned to me was that he was six months behind in his child support payments. Also, he later admitted, Donna had been allowing his parents to visit their grandchild two evenings a week—something that wasn't even mentioned-in the decree. In effect, this was a voluntary trade-off for Larry's not getting his overnight visits. Donna, of course, countered our petition with a claim for back child support and immediately cut off Larry's parents' visits.

It turned out that what was really bothering Larry—and what had inspired his counterproductive action—was the news that Donna was about to wed again. He saw red. He hadn't wanted to break up in the first place. Maybe he had even fantasized about an eventual reconciliation. Now Donna's wedding plans forced him to face the unpleasant reality. He wanted to get even. If he couldn't stop the marriage, at least he could enforce his visitation rights. Instead, he wound up worse off than before.

Who Gets Hurt and How

Legal battles after a divorce take a physical, emotional, and financial toll. People may feel that the worst is over and it's time to put the bitterness behind them and start a new life. Then, first thing they know, they're right back in court. I've seen people lose their jobs because of the amount of time that had to be taken off for court appearances. I've seen people forced to drastically reduce their living standards to pay increased child support. And I've seen people lose their health due to the emotional pressure and anxiety brought on by constant legal hassles.

Litigation over issues arising from a previous marriage can endanger a new one. Legal proceedings frequently create great emotional strain as old, ambivalent feelings surface. Resentments also may rise in the new spouse, who may become an unwitting party to the case. "Who's more important—your kids or me?" a new mate may complain in the heat of a custody battle. "We're spending all our money on legal fees; we can't even afford to take a vacation." Arguments over custody and child support undoubtedly contribute to the fact that remarriages involving stepchildren are much more likely to fail than those without stepchildren, especially when both spouses have been married before.

Children are the biggest losers in these wrangles. A child may become a pawn in a custody fight or visitation dispute, or even a victim of parental abuse or kidnapping.

The effects of postmarital problems may begin to show up on an anxious child's report card or in disturbed behavior. Forty percent of children of divorced parents experience academic or social failure within ten years after the divorce. Family tension in the wake of divorce and/or remarriage is frequently a factor in adolescent drug abuse and suicide, now the third leading cause of death among high-school and college-age youth.

Later, I'll suggest ways in which you can protect yourself and your loved ones from needless hurt.

Three Types of Post-Divorce Cases

Now let's take a brief look at three main types of legal actions that arise after divorce; I'll discuss each in more detail in subsequent chapters. (Similar types of cases may come up following unwed relationships.)

The first type involves **enforcement**. In this kind of case, one party needs the machinery of the law to force the other party to live up to the terms of a decree, order, or agreement.

A word about terminology. The words **decree, order**, and **agreement** are used somewhat interchangeably throughout this book. All three can refer to the official papers you receive when you're divorced. (The words may also refer to a determination of paternity, of custody, or of rights to child support or visitation for unwed parents.)

Sometimes a decree is based on an agreement between the parties. Sometimes, if the parties can't agree, the court imposes a settlement. Either way, the final order is just that—an order with legal force.

The second type of case involves an attempt to **modify**, or change, some aspect of the original decree, order, or agreement.

The third type of case involves an attempt to **nullify** (invalidate) a divorce or its terms.

What Sorts of Enforcement Problems Arise?

What kinds of situations might lead you to seek help in enforcing your decree, order, or agreement? I've given several examples in this chapter. Your ex may get laid off and miss alimony or child support payments or simply may skip town and refuse to pay. He or she may interfere with your custodial or visitation rights. Or your ex may fail to comply with the agreed terms for division of property—for example, to sell or deed over the family home.

How Can Your Decree Be Changed?

The largest and most varied group of cases consists of those that call for a change, or modification, of the decree.

Lawyers are fond of saying that circumstances alter cases. What if you're making hefty maintenance payments to your wife, and she takes a well-to-do lover or a high-salaried job? Are you entitled to end or reduce your contribution to her support? What if your ex, who has custody of the children, moves in with a companion of the same sex or joins a cult? What if he or she marries or begins living with someone who abuses the child? These and other factors that didn't exist at the time of the divorce might convince a judge to reconsider the question of which parent should have custody.

Perhaps issues have arisen that weren't thought through at the time of the divorce, such as who pays for the children's higher education. Some items, such as alimony, may have been reserved for future determination.

Not everything in a divorce agreement is subject to change. As a general rule, property settlements can't be modified; the only way to change the terms is through nullification. On the other hand, virtually anything that involves children— custody, visitation, support, and so on—is open to question.

Of course, almost anything in the original agreement can be modified if both parties agree. I've already referred to situations in which the parties would have been well advised to jointly seek modification of support or visitation provisions, rather than taking the law into their own hands.

How the Gender Revolution Affects Your Rights and Obligations

In most families, the man is still the chief breadwinner, so he's the one most likely to be paying alimony or child support. But nowadays the reverse may be true. The fact that most women (including more than 60 percent of wives with children under the age of 18) now work outside the home has radically revised family law. A working woman's pension rights, for example, are generally regarded as part of the marital property to be divided upon divorce. Women no longer automatically seek or get custody, especially when children are above preschool age. (More than one in ten youngsters in one-parent households now live with their fathers.) And men aren't the only ones who may face obligations of maintenance and child support.

These trends, in turn, are prompting some ex-husbands of long standing to press for more advantageous alterations to their divorce settlements. For example, in most states a woman is now expected to go out and look for work or at least to begin developing marketable skills within a reasonable time. If you've been paying alimony to your ex-wife for several years, and she's in good health but has made no effort to become self-supporting, you may find, if you consult your lawyer, that you're not necessarily locked into the terms of a decree entered at a time when the law was different—especially if the children are grown. By the same token, if you're a woman getting alimony, don't assume that will be a permanent state of affairs.

One effect of the gender revolution is the trend toward joint custody, which gives both parents the right and responsibility to oversee their children's welfare and development. One purpose is to avoid putting the children in the middle of a custody fight. Unfortunately, joint custody doesn't always work out as well as its proponents claim. We're seeing more and more suits to modify joint custody, either by altering its specific terms or by ending it and changing to sole custody.

When Can a Divorce Be Nullified?

Normally, of course, a divorce is binding. What's done can't be undone. But there are exceptions.

Fraud is one basis for nullifying a divorce settlement. You may be able to prove that your ex tricked or deceived you and the court in order to gain an unfair advantage (for example, by hiding some assets). Or you may be able to show that you were forced, pressured, or threatened, or that you were emotionally distraught or inebriated, or for whatever reason were in no condition to understand and take responsibility for what you agreed to. (It's also possible to nullify a finding of paternity—for example, if you admitted to it without being advised of your rights and of the consequences.)

Why an "Uncontested" Divorce May Not Be in Your Best Interest

I can't end this chapter without a warning about some popular approaches that seek to smooth the process of divorce but often end up causing trouble. One is the "uncontested" divorce.

Here's a typical scenario of how an uncontested divorce can go wrong: David and Elaine go into court with their lawyers for a pretrial conference to discuss the issues involved in the dissolution of their marriage. With the judge's help, they come to a meeting of the minds, making a trial unnecessary. The two lawyers orally run through the terms that have just been agreed to, while a court reporter takes them down. (This is called "proving up" the agreement.) David and Elaine swear to the agreement. The lawyers reduce it to writing, and the judge approves and signs it.

Maybe David or Elaine will later feel that he or she got a bad deal. But there's not much that can be done at that point. The court will be reluctant to disturb the agreement; all the other party's lawyer would have to do would be to pull out the transcript of the hearing and say, "See? You agreed to this under oath."

In many instances, people don't realize that once they say "yes" on the witness stand, they are bound—even though they haven't signed anything yet. It's far better, if you have any misgivings at all, to wait until you can go over the terms in writing before committing yourself.

Actually, the term "uncontested" can be a misnomer. The couple and their lawyers may have sweated and strained during court maneuvers for a year or more as the couple went through a lengthy negotiation and mediation process. The warring spouses may even have come close to blows over who would get the Royal Doulton china. But once they've come to terms, and the resulting agreement is proved up, it's officially uncontested.

When I say that an "uncontested" divorce can cause trouble, however, I'm referring not to that type of situation but to quickie divorces based on oral agreements, like David's and Elaine's, or situations where one party has been intimidated into agreement, or default judgments granted to one party in the other's absence—situations that frequently result in attempts to nullify the divorce.

No-Fault Is No Panacea

Since 1970, "no-fault" divorce laws have been adopted in some form in every state in the union. This innovation was heralded as the way to simplify divorce and to avoid the acrimony and hypocrisy inherent in the old system. But no-fault is a widely misunderstood term. No-fault laws didn't simplify divorce as much as many people think, and in fact they vary widely in different states.

In principle, no-fault is definitely an improvement over the old method of establishing grounds for divorce: no embarrassing finger-pointing, no private detectives, no lying on the witness stand to prove adultery, bigamy, or physical or mental cruelty. All a couple may have to do if they want to split up (depending on the requirements in their particular state) is to tell a judge that they have "irreconcilable differences" or are "incompatible" or that there has been an "irretrievable breakdown" in their marriage. In some states, it's not even necessary that the two have been living apart.

Obviously it's better that husbands and wives don't have to make false accusations against each other or don't have to put up with phony charges made against them in open court. But most lay people don't realize that the grounds for divorce are a separate matter from what is actually the heart of a divorce case: reaching a settlement about division of assets and decisions about child custody and support. In some states that have no-fault laws, marital misconduct can still be considered (and should be, in my opinion) in determining alimony and property division; and in all states, misconduct must be weighed in determining who gets custody.

Most relevant to the subject of this book are the potential perils of making divorce too easy. In their desire to get through the process as quickly and painlessly as possible, a couple may avoid important issues that need to be addressed and that, if not resolved, will later come back to haunt them. Burying a problem is no solution; it will only resurface. If people have differences, sooner or later a quick fix will come unglued, and they (or some creative lawyer) will find ways to litigate those differences.

Actually, the pendulum is now starting to swing in the opposite direction, toward holding people responsible for their actions. In the final chapter, I'll discuss one aspect of this trend: the question of accountability for the results of sexual conduct, from transmission of AIDS to complications of unwanted pregnancy.

Inadequate Legal Representation Is False Economy

Many people contemplating divorce feel more comfortable going to a family member or friend who happens to be a lawyer than to a stranger. They may try to save a few dollars by hiring a young, inexperienced attorney, or one who handles many different types of legal matters and is too busy to give undivided attention to the intricacies of divorce law. Some couples make a big mistake by using the same lawyer, either to cut costs or (so they think) to keep things amicable. Worse yet, some couples think they can save money and hassles by having no lawyers at all and just dealing with each other directly.

In my experience, these are the people most likely to land back in court. For an agreement to embody a fair accommodation of both parties' interests, each needs the best possible representation. I can't emphasize enough that if conflicts are thrashed out in the first place, they are less likely to crop up later.

Most people want to believe that everything is going to work out, that problems happen only to other people. But a professional who concentrates on this complex area of the law has the experience and expertise to anticipate the contingencies that could affect your rights in the future. It's your lawyer's job to call your attention not just to what probably will happen, or what might or should happen, but to the remote, one-in-a-thousand, long shot occurrence that you'd never anticipate on your own.

2

UNWED
RELATIONSHIPS:
NO EASY EXIT

If you're living with someone of the other sex who is not your husband or wife, or if you have done so, you're part of one of today's hottest trends. In 1986, there were four times as many unmarried couples living together as in 1970, and in 1988 there were 2.6 million—up 63 percent from the number in 1980.

Although these couples still represent a small proportion of all households at any given time, cohabitation is becoming an experience in which the majority of Americans engage at some point in their lives. In a random nationwide survey of 13,000 people, two sociologists at the University of Wisconsin found that 44 percent had lived with someone of the other sex before marriage. And 58 percent of those who had recently remarried said they had cohabited between marriages. The extent of the cohabitation explosion may be measured by the fact that four times as many Americans who married between 1980 and 1984 had done it than had those who married between 1965 and 1974.

These figures, of course, don't include people who have cohabited and not gotten married afterward; nor do they include homosexual couples. For some people, cohabitation becomes a more-or-less permanent way of life, either with one partner or a succession of partners.

Who Cohabits and Why?

Most couples who live together are in their twenties and thirties. A little more than half have never been married; about 40 percent are divorced or separated from their previous mates.

One factor in this lifestyle choice is the tendency to postpone marriage or not to marry at all. Many young people who are physically mature want and need sexual intimacy but don't feel ready for marriage—either because they are in college, pursuing advanced or professional degrees, or just getting started in careers, or because they don't feel emotionally prepared to make a permanent commitment. Then, too, a person who has been burned by a bad marriage may want to test out a new relationship to avoid repeating the mistake. (Ironically, according to the University of Wisconsin study, people who have cohabited before marriage are more, not less, likely to divorce; in fact, they are almost twice as likely.)

How Lovers Become Legally Entangled

Getting into an unwed relationship may be fairly simple, but getting out can be far more complicated and costly than many people realize, and the aftereffects may extend far into the future.

Most cohabitants enter into their live-in arrangements with little premeditation. For example: Sally and Nick meet at a singles bar. They hit it off and end up at Nick's place. The next day, Nick asks Sally over for a quiet dinner. By the end of the week, she's moved in. Chances are that neither of them has given much thought to what problems could arise later on. Things may get sticky if Sally wants to move out or if Nick wants her to—especially if they've shared not only a bed but furniture purchases, a bank account, and maybe even a child.

The issues Nick and Sally will face if and when they decide to split up may depend in part on what state they live in and how long they have lived together. Common law (or de facto) marriage, in which a couple who cohabit for a number of years take on the same legal rights and responsibilities as if they were married, has been abolished in most states. Where it still exists, couples who live together on a continuing basis and present themselves to the community as if they were married may have to get a decree to end their relationship, just as if they were dissolving a marriage. In all other states, the status of unwed partners is far less clear.

Litigation following the ending of an intimate relationship generally falls into two categories: (1) cases involving enforcement of a live-in agreement or implied contract, usually having to do with division of property or maintenance (popularly known as "palimony"); and (2) cases involving children.

Is Your Live-In Agreement Binding?

In *Hearts and Dollars*, I explained why a written live-in agreement between two unmarried people who share a household (whether they are of the same or different sexes) is a good idea, and why it's important to have it drafted properly. While a court may or may not enforce such an agreement, a judge is far more likely to do so than if the relationship is based solely on an unwritten understanding or a document you've concocted yourselves.

A live-in agreement, to be legally binding, must have the elements of any valid contract. First, it must involve mutual consideration; that is, each party must provide something of value. For example, Sally and Nick might agree that he will provide the groceries, she will do the cooking, and they will split the rent. Second, the agreement must be negotiated at arm's length, between two people who are dealing with each other in good faith and with their eyes open. Finally, the agreement must not be contrary to public policy; that is, it must not involve violation of law. Courts tend to look askance at live-in agreements based on sexual relations alone as tantamount to prostitution.

There's a good chance that an agreement that meets the conditions I've just outlined will hold up in court.

When Unwed Partners Own or Rent Property Together

Live-in lovers often undertake joint financial obligations that can be hard to untangle after a breakup. When an unmarried couple co-sign a lease or mortgage papers, for example, both people are legally bound.

Suppose Nick moves out, and even though he co-signed the lease, he refuses to pay any more rent. Sally can sue him, but for all practical purposes, if she can't pay the rent herself, she'll probably face eviction. And the landlord can go after either Sally or Nick, or both, for the unpaid rent.

It's best to anticipate such problems in a carefully drawn non-marital agreement. For example, such an agreement might provide that in the event of a breakup, one party will be responsible for the lease and the other will vacate the premises within thirty days. The one taking over the lease would agree to hold the other party harmless for any obligations under that document. In other words, if Sally had agreed to assume the lease obligation and the landlord sued Nick for the unpaid rent, Nick could in turn sue and collect from Sally—that is, if she had any assets that could be turned into cash.

If Nick and Sally owned their place together, the best bet would be to sell it and divide the equity according to who put up what proportion of the money. If they were joint tenants, either one would need the other's signature in order to sell.

Can You Get Palimony?

When cohabitants have no written agreement, one of them may claim that there was an implied contract—that is, a contract implied by the parties' actions or expectations. This brings us to the question of palimony.

Strictly speaking, there's no such thing as palimony. No statute mentions the word. Except in the few states that still recognize common law marriages, no court will order an ex-cohabitant to make maintenance payments to the rejected partner just because they have lived together. There are, however, a growing number of cases expanding on rights of cohabitants in implied contracts.

"Palimony" is a catchy term coined during the sensational suit by Michelle Triola against film actor Lee Marvin. Lee allegedly promised to support Michelle for life if she would give up her singing career, move in with him, and perform the "duties" of a wife. She did, and even changed her name to Marvin. Several years later, Michelle claimed, he dumped her. But California's highest court found no implied contract.

Since then, other women (and some men, too) have pressed for palimony from former lovers—both straight and gay—with the help of sharp lawyers, and courts and legislatures are still struggling with the issues involved. Palimony suits involving celebrities like Hugh Hefner, Billie Jean King, and Liberace have received tremendous notoriety. But these cases haven't made clear law; in fact, many of them never reached the courts. The recent suit filed against Hefner by his four-year live-in, Carrie Leigh, is a good example. She sued, he countersued, then the case was dropped; yet the headlines went on.

No one, then, should enter into a live-in relationship with the expectation of getting palimony after the party's over. But cohabitants may have some recourse if they can show that they had an implied contract.

Although precedents vary, courts generally look with more favor on a claim based on the economic aspects of a relationship than on a claim based on the sexual aspects. (For an implied contract to be enforceable—as with a written one—it must not violate public policy, which generally frowns on sexual services as contractual consideration.) If Michelle Marvin, for example, had been able to prove that she had contributed to the relationship in some financially measurable form, the outcome of her case might have been different.

The Illinois Supreme Court, in the case of *Spafford v. Coats*, held that Donna Spafford was entitled to get back her share of the value of cars that she and her live-in partner, Richard Coats, had bought in his name. The court reasoned that Coats would be unjustly enriched if he were able to keep property that Spafford had helped pay for.

A cohabitant might establish an implied contract by regularly putting paychecks into a joint account or by performing unpaid work. A woman I represent lived with a man for twenty years and worked in his restaurant without pay. He promised to take care of her in his will, but when he died, she found that he had left her nothing. What's more, his family threw her out of the house the couple had lived in. Now she's suing them for the value of her contribution to the business as well as to the relationship with the deceased man. And she stands a good chance to collect.

When Children Are Involved

According to some estimates, one out of every five children born today is born out of wedlock. In 1986, more than one-fourth of the 14.8 million children in single-parent households lived with a parent who had never married. In addition, about 800,000 children were living with unmarried couples (though it's possible that some of these were children from one partner's previous marriage).

In many ways, cases involving unwed parents are similar to those that arise after divorce. Most of the principles I outlined in chapter 1 (and will expand on later) may apply to unwed parents, too. Custody battles, conflicts over visitation rights, and child support enforcement problems involve ex-lovers as well as ex-spouses.

Paternity and Child Support

If you're an unwed mother, you're far less likely to get adequate—or any—support money from the child's father than if you had been married to him. In 1986, according to the U.S. Bureau of the Census, only 18 percent of never-married mothers living with children whose fathers were absent had been awarded child support, compared with 74 percent of other women in that position. The average amount of child support actually received by never-married women who were awarded it was less than half that received by divorced women. Also, unmarried mothers had a much poorer chance of having health insurance included in their awards; only 24 percent got it, as compared with 46 percent of other women.

Why the difference? First of all, in order to get money for child support, an unwed mother must establish paternity; that is, she must get a court order declaring that a particular man is the child's father. Paternity cases frequently are handled much like criminal cases; the alleged father is the defendant, and the mother is the plaintiff. The mother is often represented by a public prosecutor rather than by a private lawyer, because historically the state had an interest in going after the father to support his child, who might otherwise become (or already was) a recipient of public aid.

However, much of the time the father can't be located; so, even if a finding of paternity is made, he can't be ordered to pay child support. The public prosecutor's office (the state's attorney's office in many jurisdictions) is generally a pretty busy place, and women often have to cope with red tape or a quick shuffle. Also, because state paternity laws vary widely, it may be difficult to establish paternity if the parents live in different states.

Some cases are "lost" by never being filed; census data show that nearly one-half of unwed mothers without child support awards didn't seek awards. Why not? It's my observation that even though a mother's marital status is supposed to make no difference in her eligibility for child support, many women in this position feel guilty or lack the confidence to push for what they are entitled to. Or they may feel that they are capable of raising their children by themselves and may not want the fathers to be involved in their lives.

Paternity Suits Are Proliferating

While paternity is established in fewer than one-third of the approximately 800,000 out-of-wedlock births each year, the number of paternity cases in United States courts has swelled to more than 250,000. Even a one-night stand often leads to a paternity suit.

A significant loosening of restrictions on the period of time in which a paternity suit must be filed has opened the floodgates to a rush of new cases. In the past, a man could escape paternal responsibility unless suit was brought before the child was two, three, or four years old, depending on the particular state's statute of limitations. Now federal law requires states to permit the establishment of paternity until the child reaches majority: in some states, age 18, in others, 21. In addition, some states, such as Colorado, tack on an additional period beyond the age of majority by letting the normal statute of limitations begin to run at that time.

What's more, the change may be held to apply to previously adjudicated cases. That means that if a woman's suit was dismissed as untimely under an old statute of limitations, she may now be able to sue again. One mother, who had filed when the child was four years old only to be told that she was too late, filed again when the child was 10, after the change in the law. This time, she was awarded child support—retroactively.

Furthermore, in many states a youngster himself or herself can bring a paternity claim. This is true in those states that have adopted the Uniform Parentage Act, which defines parental rights and obligations to a child regardless of whether or not the parents are married. Under this act, a teenager can bring a paternity claim up to two years after the age of 18.

In one such case I handled, the mother had settled with the father for $20,000 and a finding of nonpaternity. He thought he was off the hook. The mother spent the money on herself. Then, when the daughter was 17 and wanted to go to college, she asked me to reopen the case. I filed a lawsuit on her behalf, arguing that the mother had no right to sign away the daughter's claim to support. We won, and the disgruntled father had to pay his daughter's tuition bills.

Proving Paternity

A second reason for the increase in paternity cases—and part of the rationale for extending the statutes of limitations—is the advent of new, highly reliable scientific methods of establishing parentage. In the past, if a man took a blood test, the test could be used to prove that he was not the father, but not to establish that he was. That was because the accuracy of the tests was too uncertain to force a man to assume a child support obligation. Now a more sophisticated blood test called HLA can, when taken together with other evidence, establish with as high as 99 percent probability that a man is the father.

Unlike the old blood tests, which merely identified groups of people with similar blood types, the HLA test detects a complex combination of enzymes, proteins, and antigens in the child's blood and matches these with the makeup of the alleged father's blood. If the two don't match in any respect, the man can't be the father. If they match exactly, a formula called the paternity index is used to calculate the relative statistical likelihood that he, rather than some other randomly selected man, would have produced a child with that particular combination of inherited blood characteristics.

In most states, the HLA test is now admissible in evidence not only to disprove paternity but to help establish it. A man may be required to take the test, and the results, regardless of the outcome, may be put into evidence. Still, the test can't establish with absolute certainty that a particular man is the father of a particular child; and unless that point is clearly understood, HLA test results can be misleading.

DNA "fingerprinting" is another powerful new tool to help determine parentage. This system, which has been used in British courts to identify crime suspects, was introduced in the United States in 1987.

DNA fingerprinting relies upon genetic characteristics that are unique to the individual. DNA molecules (the substance of the genes that determine all of our inherited traits) are extracted from one or two drops of blood or a trace of semen and then are separated into a distinctive pattern (resembling the bar codes on products sold in grocery stores), which shows up on X-ray film. Half of a child's pattern matches the mother's; the other half, the father's.

These new technologies encourage the filing of paternity suits because of the increased likelihood of success. Before, the standard defense was to attack the woman's reputation. A man's lawyer might bring in five other men with whom she had engaged in sexual relations, so as to plant doubt in the jury's minds as to who was the actual father. Women hesitated to file paternity suits because they dreaded having their past sexual encounters paraded before the jury. But with scientific means of identifying the father, such tactics are outmoded.

No Excuses: The Father Is the Father

Once a man has been proven to be the biological father, he has few, if any, legal defenses to a claim for child support.

As the stigma of unwed motherhood recedes, some unmarried women who feel their biological clocks ticking away are making a conscious choice to have babies. It's becoming almost chic for a woman to say, "I'm 35 and I don't have a husband, but I want to be a mother before it's too late." In some instances, the woman is quite up-front about her intentions. She needs a man to help her make a baby, and then she wants him to get out of the picture and leave her to raise her child.

In other cases, though, the woman is less forthright. She may pretend she is sterile or on the Pill. "Don't worry—it's safe," she whispers soothingly; the next thing the man knows, he's socked with a paternity suit. If he's biologically the father, the fact that she misled him is no defense. It doesn't matter whether he was duped, drugged, or seduced; he's still legally responsible for the child.

I have a male client who is 72 years old and half-senile. A 38-year-old professional woman lured him into having sex with her and then bore a baby who has Down's syndrome. This man doesn't even remember the incident. But his HLA blood test came out positive, and now he must support a retarded child.

To a marked extent, paternity law, which used to be biased against the woman, has become pro-female and pro-child. The morality of the woman is no longer a factor. Whether she set up the man is irrelevant. The fact that she has the choice whether to go through with the birth or have an abortion doesn't enter in. If the father is the father, that's all that counts. The pendulum may swing back, of course; but as of now, courts are insisting that the biological father assume at least partial financial responsibility for the life he wittingly or unwittingly helped bring into the world.

The conclusion of a paternity suit, or even of the father's life, may not be the end of the matter. The Supreme Court has held that an illegitimate child can file a claim against a father's estate after the man has died. To forestall any such development, I sometimes suggest to my male clients that they may wish to put in their wills a clause specifically disinheriting any illegitimate children they may have.

Men Bring Paternity Suits Too

A man bringing a paternity suit may seem like a contradiction in terms. But it happens fairly often. In a reverse paternity case, a father seeks to establish his relationship to the child so as to assert his parental rights.

A woman may say, "I had the kid, and I don't want you to have any part of it. I don't want your money, and I don't want you. Just stay out of our lives." The man, however, may decide that he wants to see and support his child. If blood testing identifies him as the father, he can get court-ordered visitation rights. Or he may seek and obtain custody if the facts indicate that it's in the child's best interest.

Mothers Don't Automatically Have Custody

Most women who have had babies out of wedlock make the mistake of thinking that they automatically have custody. There is no custody without a court decree.

Sometimes, after the mother has been raising the child for years, the father will come in and claim custody. He may even "kidnap" the child, and because the mother doesn't have legal custody, a complex custody battle may ensue.

Even if a woman doesn't want to bring a paternity action, doesn't care about getting child support, or doesn't know where the father is, if she intends to raise her child, she should seek custody at the outset. That way, if the father later brings a reverse paternity suit and tries to get custody, he must seek a change of custody, and his burden of proof will be greater than for an original custody order.

Breaking Up an Unwed Relationship Can Be Stormier Than Breaking Up a Marriage

Now you can begin to see why an unwed relationship can be a legal time bomb. Things may seem to be going smoothly—even the split-up may seem amicable—but suddenly, maybe years later, a palimony claim, paternity suit, or custody fight may ensue.

One disturbing feature of such combat is that you may be battling with a virtual stranger. Post-divorce litigation is distressing enough, but at least your opponent is a known adversary—someone you presumably once respected and cared deeply about and who respected and cared deeply about you. That may or may not be true of an unwed relationship.

Another complication is that such relationships are often clandestine. A married man who has had an affair may be afraid to have anything to do with his illegitimate child for fear his indiscretion will be found out; his former mistress may keep the threat of a potential lawsuit hanging over him for years. A married woman who bears another man's child may lead her husband to believe that he's the biological father, and her husband may never know that he's supporting someone else's child.

To Sum Up

- If you're cohabiting or planning to do so, have a lawyer draw up a live-in agreement involving an exchange of consideration (something of value) other than sex.
- If you live in a common law state, be aware that cohabiting for a certain period of time may confer upon you and your partner the rights and responsibilities of marriage.
- To establish an implied live-in contract, be able to show that you contributed financially to the relationship or did unpaid work. Check with your lawyer if you think you may have a claim.
- If you're an unwed mother and plan to raise your child, be sure to get a court order giving you custody. Be assertive about claiming paternity and child support.

•If you're a man in an unwed relationship, you may want to put a clause in your will disinheriting any illegitimate children you may have.

3

IS YOUR EX
HARASSING YOU?

When Donna opens the envelope containing her monthly child support check, she cringes; her ex, Doug, invariably has decorated the check with a symbolic drop of his blood.

Jim's ex, Elaine, suspects he has some cash stashed away that he managed to hide during the property settlement. She calls the Internal Revenue Service to report him for alleged nonpayment of taxes.

Barbara is awakened at 4:00 AM by the insistent ringing of her telephone. She picks it up in terror, knowing who the caller will be. "You whore," whispers her ex, Brian, "I'm gonna break your legs."

These scenarios are examples of the harassment that often goes on between former spouses or lovers. Harassment—which, legally, means interfering with someone's personal liberty—may be verbal or physical, intentional or unintentional, direct or indirect. It may range from minor baiting and belittling to rows so serious that the police should be called. It may take the form of repeated telephoning; hanging around the ex's house; tearing up his mail instead of forwarding it; pestering her family; spreading rumors and gossip about him; running her down in front of the children or mutual friends; disrupting his business; following her lover; finding excuses for nuisance litigation; or threatening her with bodily harm.

In my experience, harassment is probably the most pervasive problem in divorce and post-divorce cases. Badgering, spying, threatening, and fighting are common during divorce proceedings, and often the decree doesn't halt the hostilities, especially if one or both parties believe they got a raw deal. Unwed intimacy, too—as the movie *Fatal Attraction* dramatically portrays—can have menacing consequences. Although the woman in that film turned out to be a psychopath, the urge for revenge when a person feels wronged is quite normal.

"Till Death ..."

Psychologists say there are deeper reasons for harassment. Tenderness and rage are two sides of the same coin, and the pain of parting often causes it to flip over.

Although harassers may believe they are simply getting even for injustices, harassment is often a tip-off that one or both parties don't really want to end the relationship. They just can't seem to leave each other alone. Although the legal and physical bonds have been broken, the emotional bonds are still there. For example, a man who can't accept the breakup of his marriage may act as if the rift had never occurred. Instead of just picking up the children on visitation days, he'll walk around the house, open the refrigerator, and check out the situation, until his ex is ready to jump out of her skin. This sort of behavior, if nothing is done to stop it, can go on for years. It's a way to get a response from the other person; a sign that the relationship is still alive.

Harassment may be a way to deal with the pain of rejection and the resulting loss of self-esteem. A woman whose ex left her may become obsessed with thinking up ways to humiliate and annoy him. She may call his office regularly, keep his receptionist tied up on the line, and threaten to come to the office unless he drops what he's doing and gets on the phone.

Keeping the Upper Hand

Harassment may be a way for one person to demonstrate continued control over the other, even if that control consists of no more than the power to irritate. It's easy for one ex to push the button that drives the other crazy. No one knows a person's weak spots better than someone who has lived with that person. Like siblings, each knows how to goad the other.

According to some psychologists, authoritarian men with low self-esteem and traditional ideas about male dominance tend to show this need for control—which (ironically) may show itself in a loss of self-control. If the woman initiated the break, the man, seeing her "rebellion" as a challenge to his manhood, may explode, justifying his violent behavior by the need to "punish" her.

In one case, which took a bizarre turn, a couple argued bitterly over who should get the family dog. The man seized the animal. The court ordered him to give it to his ex-wife. He complied, all right: he strangled the dog and dropped it on her doorstep.

Some psychologists explain harassment as an expression of anger and frustration when an emotional bond is severed. According to this theory, the more harassers strive for the upper hand, the more they betray their emotional dependence. That's why they persist in trying to meet their ex-mates or ex-lovers, provoke them, and get a rise out of them.

Harassment rises sharply during holiday periods, when sentimental images torment the unattached, leaving them especially vulnerable. A woman who knows how important it is to her ex to spend Thanksgiving with the children may make excuses to prevent him from doing so.

Children Suffer

Children who become pawns in their parents' power struggles are the real victims. A man whose wife had divorced him sent his son a single ice skate for Christmas. A father who hadn't seen his ten-year-old son for four years wanted to resume the relationship. His ex reminded the boy that his father had punished him severely when he was younger, and the youngster became so fearful of a reunion that he began wetting his bed. Lasting psychological damage, teenage delinquency, and inability to relate well to the opposite sex have been attributed to such parental machinations.

According to psychologist Mark L. Goldstein, a family therapist and school psychologist who teaches child development at the University of Illinois College of Medicine in Chicago, when a marriage breaks up because of another man or woman— not simply because the marital relationship itself isn't working—the two parents almost always end up fighting over the child, who becomes a vehicle for revenge. "These parents want to get back at the spouse not just for leaving them but for leaving them for someone else," Goldstein explains.

Support checks and visitation are natural arenas for conflict because they are legally-sanctioned contact points between the parents. A custodial parent may be completely inflexible about visiting times, may call at the last minute to change the time of pickup, or may fail to have the child ready as agreed. A noncustodial parent may be habitually late, may cancel at the last minute, or may simply fail to show up, leaving an annoyed ex to scratch personal plans and deal with disappointed youngsters. Children caught in these power games often imagine that they are to blame ("I was bad, so Daddy doesn't come anymore," or, "If I was a good girl, Mommy wouldn't cry so much").

One father missed his scheduled visiting day for three weeks in a row. His ex had gone to great pains to arrange to have the children ready at the appointed time. She was livid but could do nothing: her ex-husband was entitled to visitation but couldn't be forced to do it. (To eliminate that quirk in the law, I believe visitation rights should be subject to termination if either party willfully and repeatedly abuses or fails to exercise them.)

In theory, joint (or shared) custody is supposed to forestall such hassles, and sometimes it does. But not necessarily. Joint custody may be used as leverage by an angry ex or may merely generate more opportunities for conflict.

It Can Happen To the Nicest People

As I mentioned in chapter 1, an "uncontested" or quickie divorce may have an unexpectedly bitter aftermath. A couple may want to avoid a messy court fight and stay friends. They may even use the same lawyer. As a result, they never really address issues that may later erupt in the form of harassment.

Sometimes a change in circumstances dramatically alters an apparently amicable post-divorce relationship, tapping into deep-seated emotions and bringing to the surface a festering sense of loss and resentment. A woman who finds out that her ex-husband plans to remarry may threaten to "tell all" to his new partner. A man may suddenly become "difficult" when his ex moves in with another man.

Irene and Bill had a "friendly" divorce. Six months later, she wanted to go away for a weekend. Bill agreeably offered to take the children. Irene then happened to mention that her plans included her current "friend," Craig. At the eleventh hour, Bill called to say that something had come up and he couldn't help her out after all. Irene couldn't find a babysitter and had to cancel her trip. Chances are that Bill's change of heart had more to do with his unresolved feelings for Irene (and his desire to punish her for preferring another man to him) than with inability to spend time with his children.

Harassment Can Become Violent

Although harassment may be no more than a petty annoyance, sometimes it's much more serious. It's not surprising that men and women who abuse their spouses during marriage, or their lovers while they are living together, would continue to do so, given the chance, after the relationship ends. Nor is it surprising that a society in which violence is glorified on movie and television screens has a chilling rate of domestic violence.

A national telephone survey by Louis Harris and Associates in 1985 found that physical violence occurs among more than one out of six married couples in the United States. There are some 1.6 million households in which husbands punch, bite, or kick their wives, and an even greater number of households in which women severely assault their husbands (perhaps in some cases in retaliation or self-defense). Since the 1970s, the battered women's movement has done much to expose and ameliorate the plight of battered women at all levels of society, but the problem of battered men is just beginning to be recognized.

A national survey of nearly 6,000 couples, released in mid-1988 by a University of New Hampshire sociologist, found violence occurring among 14 percent of the married and a shocking 35 percent of unmarried cohabitants. Physical abuse often goes hand in hand with emotional or psychological abuse, and the two reinforce each other. A person who becomes accustomed to being humiliated or put down may lose self-confidence and become an easier target for battering.

Who Is Likely To Become Violent?

Psychologists say that a person who keeps anger bottled up or who was abused as a child, or a man who has an exaggerated need to "wear the pants in the family," is likely to have a low boiling point. Unfortunately, the signs of incipient violence are often overlooked until it's too late. And the violence isn't always directed against the real target of anger but may spill over and hurt innocent bystanders.

That happened in the tragic case of 30-year-old Laurie Dann, who, in May 1988, about a year after her unwanted divorce, shot several children (one of them fatally) in a Winnetka, Illinois school and then killed herself.

Reporters trying to piece together the story of Laurie Dann's descent into madness found that her acquaintances remembered such seemingly harmless signs of mental disturbance as opening a car door at stoplights; tapping her foot on the pavement; tiptoeing around a carpet; refusing to close kitchen cabinets or to touch metal; recoiling from human touch; wearing gloves or compulsively scrubbing her hands; and constantly riding elevators. Her strange behavior turned menacing with the failure of her marriage. During and after the divorce proceedings, she allegedly made some 150 threatening phone calls to her

Box 1

Warning Signs of Harassment

Harassment often starts with small, apparently trivial incidents and gets progressively uglier. Here are some early warning signs to watch for. Does your ex:

•Take an inordinate interest in your love life?

•Call you more than once a day "to check on the kids," or call you frequently at work?

•Call you and hang up? (If you think it's your ex, it probably is.)

•Appear at your home other than at visitation times?

•Fail to return your children's clothes or toys after visitation?

•Habitually send your support payments late for no apparent reason, or fail to pay bills he's responsible for?

•Gossip about you to your friends and relatives?

•Try to get the children on his or her side by making frequent derogatory remarks about you? (Look for changes in the children's behavior that may indicate that they are being brainwashed.)

•Use the children to relay threats? (One father, every time he picked up his son for visitation, was greeted with "Mom says we're gonna move away, and you're never gonna see us again.")

ex-husband, Russell Dann, and his family (as well as to an ex-boyfriend) and (according to Russell) stabbed him with an ice pick while he was asleep.

According to news stories, when the ice pick attack and some of the phone calls were reported to law enforcement authorities, Laurie Dann made countercharges that her ex-husband had raped her, robbed her, and set her house afire. Russell Dann failed a lie detector test regarding the ice pick incident, and police found insufficient evidence to press charges about the phone calls.

Russell Dann hired private investigators to document his ex-wife's increasingly unstable behavior, which reportedly included slashing furniture in homes where she was babysitting, leaving raw meat around to rot, and making explosives. But, according to the *Chicago Tribune*, only once during a year and a half of surveillance did the investigators take their information to the police. Furthermore, although Laurie Dann was under intermittent psychiatric care, no steps were taken to have her committed to a mental hospital. And, in part because she had no history of institutionalization, she was able to legally purchase three guns. Despite her father's informal assurance to police that they would be kept in a safe deposit box, she clearly had access to them. Perhaps if the victims of Laurie Dann's harassment had been more insistent in calling her behavior to the attention of authorities, the Winnetka tragedy might have been averted.

What Can You Do If You're Being Harassed?

Your first impulse may be to take your ex to court. But (as with Laurie Dann) harassment can be hard to prove; usually it's one person's word against the other's. Also, defining what is and isn't harassment may be difficult. Is it harassment when a woman calls her ex-husband at the office, or could there be a valid reason? Is a man withholding or delaying child support payments to get even with his ex or because he's having financial troubles? Furthermore, there's seldom one clearly guilty party; typically, both join in a vicious cycle of provocation, retaliation, and response. ("You won't let me see Johnny today? Wait and see how soon you get your next support check!")

With indirect harassment involving, for example, support payments and visitation, there are legal steps you can take, which I'll discuss in the appropriate chapters. But when it comes to direct harassment, legal remedies often seem disproportionate to the offense, and judges are reluctant to impose them. Should a man be fined or thrown in jail for calling his wife six times in one day? The conduct has to be very clear and pretty outrageous for a judge to take that step.

Then, too, a harassment suit (as judges well know) may itself be a form of harassment. One woman, who had been married to a prominent politician, charged her ex with beating her up. The evidence: pictures of her with two black eyes. It turned out upon investigation that the photos had been taken shortly after her cosmetic surgery. But the story had already hit the newspapers, and the damage to the man's reputation was done. To this day, he's "the guy who beat his wife." Although the charges were dropped, she got what she wanted: she embarrassed him publicly.

Psychological counseling is probably the best way to get to the root of a harassment problem. But how do you get your ex to go? You might try asking your lawyer to suggest it to his or her lawyer, but don't hold your breath waiting for it to happen.

That doesn't mean there's nothing you can do. If you're being victimized, you can and should take control of what's happening to you. (See Box 2 for some practical tips.) For example, I had a client who was paying child support to his ex-wife. Meanwhile, she was constantly taunting him with offhand remarks like, "How do you know the kid is yours?" Finally he got fed up with her verbal abuse. Furthermore, he began to suspect that maybe he wasn't actually the father. He eventually took a blood test, and it turned out that he wasn't. As a result, he got back all of the support money he had paid. So if you can't handle the situation yourself, call your attorney and/or the police.

When Should You Call the Police?

A successful business executive came to his ex-wife's home during his visitation day to pick up a change of clothing for his

Box 2

Tips for Dealing with Harassment

- To discourage phone calls, get an answering machine. Your ex soon will tire of leaving messages. Like obscene callers, harassers get their jollies from talking to their victims. They don't get the same charge out of talking to a machine.

- Ignore minor provocations. Instead of responding emotionally, try to understand your ex's anger. Don't respond in kind. If your ex wants to continue the relationship at any cost, you play into his or her hands by reacting. It's hard to fight with someone who doesn't fight back.

- Examine your own behavior to see if you may be doing something to contribute to the problem.

- Let your ex know that you see through his or her shenanigans. A well-timed remark may take the "fun" out of the harassment game.

- If you've been seriously threatened, ask your lawyer to seek a court order restraining your ex from abusing or harassing you or your family members or from taking or destroying your property. (In some states, such an "order of protection" is issued automatically when someone files for divorce or separation.) Carry the order with you and file a certified copy with the local police. In my experience, if you put a threat on record, the other person will go out of his or her way to prove you're wrong and will never carry out the threat. You can also get an order of protection to stop harassment that's already occurring.

•Don't dismiss a disturbing incident as "minor." At the first inkling of trouble, don't let your ex in the house. Be firm and consistent. On visitation days, have the children ready at the door. If your ex tries to enter by force, call the police.

•Consult an attorney about filing a civil suit for money damages if you've been physically or emotionally abused. (Such suits—which may compensate you for your injuries, medical bills, loss of wages or earning capacity, pain and suffering, shame and humiliation, and damage to property—are allowed in some states. You may also be able to get punitive damages: a monetary award to punish the perpetrator, over and above the value of any actual damages you have sustained.) Document your injuries with photographs, medical records, and police reports.

•For help or advice, contact the National Commission Against Domestic Violence, a grass-roots organization in Washington, D.C. This organization can refer you to an agency in your state with a 24-hour hotline.

son. As the mother opened the door and handed him an outfit from the laundry basket she was holding, he grabbed the basket and dumped it on the front lawn. "Don't you have any clean clothes for the kid?" he said mockingly.

The woman called me two days later to ask what she should have done. "I was embarrassed to call the police just because he dumped out some laundry," she said. As a matter of fact, that was exactly what she should have done, and I told her so. At the very least, police interrogation and the possible attendant publicity might have discouraged a repeat performance.

Some women hesitate to call police because they are afraid of angering the man and making matters worse. But a 1986 report by statisticians in the U.S. Department of Justice found that when police are called in to stop domestic violence (whether on the part of spouses or ex-spouses), there is less likelihood of a recurrence.

The four-year national sampling included 1,437 cases of rape, robbery, and assault on women by relatives or persons well known to the victim, representing an estimated 2.1 million actual cases. Forty percent of the attacks were committed by spouses, 19 percent by ex-spouses, and 10 percent by boyfriends or ex-boyfriends.

The researchers found that nearly half of such incidents aren't reported to police, usually because the woman considers the matter private or because of fear of reprisal. They also found that about one-third of the women who are victims of domestic violence are victimized again within six months.

Now, here's the key finding: when a woman does call the police, she's 41 percent less likely to be assaulted again by her spouse or ex-spouse. Furthermore, when a second attack does occur after police involvement, it tends to be no more serious than a subsequent attack on a woman who did not call the police the first time. Thus it seems that women who are victims of domestic violence have much to gain and little to lose by dialing 911.

Will the Police Do Anything?

One reason for many women's hesitancy to call police is that they doubt the authorities can or will do anything to help them. Traditionally, arrests have been made in only about four percent of domestic disturbance calls, even though violence occurs in one-third to two-thirds of these incidents. One reason that police may have been reluctant to act was that such arrests rarely led to convictions.

But this situation is changing, in part because of the women's movement. State laws and local police department policies favoring arrest have been adopted in many states.

As of January 1987, laws in six states—Connecticut, Louisiana, Maine, Nevada, Oregon, and Washington—made arrest mandatory in domestic violence cases with or without a prior court order restraining violence, and in four states— Delaware, Minnesota, North Carolina, and Wisconsin—with such an order. In addition, 31 states and the District of Columbia had laws specifically providing for arrest at the officer's discretion in certain situations, while 13 states followed common law principles for discretionary arrest. Some of these laws specifically mention violation of orders against harassment by ex-spouses or persons who formerly lived together.

Two 1985 cases, which resulted in large monetary awards when police failed to act on complaints, have been a spur to swifter police response. In a Connecticut case, a battered ex-wife got $2.3 million for herself and $300,000 for her three-year-old son. Police had ignored her complaints that her ex-husband was violating a restraining order, and he subsequently attacked her while the little boy watched helplessly. In a New York case, a woman received $2 million after her ex assaulted their six-year-old daughter following police assurances that they would look into her complaint that he was violating a protective order.

In a widely heralded settlement of a class action lawsuit, the Dallas Police Department in May 1987 agreed not to avoid arrests in cases of alleged family violence, including incidents involving former spouses or unwed parents. Under the terms of the settlement, police are to give family violence calls high priority, respond to them as diligently as to other types of calls, treat all such reports as alleged criminal conduct, check on whether there are any applicable court orders, and make an arrest whenever "probable cause" exists; that is, when a person of ordinary intelligence who was confronted with the evidence would consider it more probable than not that an offense had occurred. In determining whether to make an arrest, police are specifically prohibited from considering such factors as whether or not the suspect and the victim are married or have cohabited and whether or not the victim has previously called police.

Don't Be a Victim

If you're a victim of harassment, even the best advice won't help you unless you make up your mind not to allow yourself to be victimized. Too often victims of harassment back off because they believe they can't do anything about it. The meek may inherit the earth someday, but in the meantime, they're likely to get hassled.

Let's face it: the legal system is far from perfect. Here, as elsewhere, it's generally the squeaky wheel that gets greased. If you're a victim, you have to let people know it. Be assertive. Don't take no for an answer. Say to yourself, "I'm important, my rights are important, and I'm not going to quit until I get some action." If the police won't listen, go to the public prosecutor. If that doesn't work, try your local newspaper or TV station, or call your representative on the city council, in the state legislature, or in Congress. Go over somebody's head or go around someone. Eventually, if you're persistent enough, you'll get relief.

"Don't be a victim" is good advice not only when you're faced with harassment but in every other aspect of your relationship with your ex. As you'll see in part 2, it's a mental set that will stand you in good stead in protecting your property settlement, collecting maintenance and child support payments to which you're entitled, and enforcing your visitation rights. In other words, it will help you get what's coming to you.

PART II

How To Get What's Coming To You

4

PROTECTING YOUR PROPERTY SETTLEMENT

Sarah thought she had made a pretty good deal with her ex. Under the settlement agreement, which was incorporated into their divorce decree, the house and its contents were hers, she was entitled to half of his pension plan plus health insurance, and she received a hefty amount of cash—in addition to a generous monthly alimony award for the first two years.

Several years later, Sarah remarried. Her new husband was transferred out of state, so she sold the house. Imagine her surprise when, at the closing, the buyer's attorney told her, "We can't close this deal! Your ex-husband's name is still on the title."

"That's impossible!" cried Sarah. "I got the house in my settlement agreement."

"That may be," the attorney replied, "but apparently your ex-husband never signed his interest over to you, so technically you're still co-owners."

Sarah seemed to be up a creek. She had completely lost track of her ex after the alimony payments stopped; she had no idea how to even begin to locate him. In fact, she had tried to contact him about a different matter a few months back with no success. As far as she knew, he could have been dead.

How could this have happened? On paper, Sarah had indeed done well in her divorce negotiations. Consider the following facts:

•According to census data, less than 36 percent of divorced women are awarded a property settlement at all. Of those, 74 percent get nonmonetary property only (such as a house, car, or furniture); about 22 percent get a one-time cash payment; and a mere 4 percent get a combination of the two, as Sarah did.

•Only one out of four women awarded property settlements also receives alimony and/or child support.

•Even fewer women—only 14 percent—without property settlements get support payments. And the average total income of women without property settlements is lower than that of women who do get them.

All in all, compared with many ex-wives, Sarah was right to consider herself fortunate. But, as the saying goes, there's many a slip 'twixt the cup and the lip. Being awarded property doesn't necessarily mean that you'll actually get it. In fact, your property settlement may be worthless unless certain steps are taken to ensure that you get what you bargained for.

In this chapter, I'll point out a few of the pitfalls that can come between you and the property that's due you, and I'll discuss some ways in which you can avoid these pitfalls.

Executing the Provisions

Most agreements have, in the fine print, a clause requiring the parties to take whatever actions are necessary to execute (carry out) the contractual provisions. A good lawyer will follow up and make sure that the parties actually do the things they are supposed to do.

Too many lawyers, however, drop a case after the judgment is entered. They'll say, "Here's your decree, thanks for the fee," and the separate document necessary to transfer ownership of the house or the car is never signed or recorded with the proper county or state office. Or the forms necessary to change the names on a bank account or to assure you of continued insurance coverage are never filed.

Luckily, in Sarah's case it turned out that there was a self-executing clause in her decree. (Such a provision can be built in to make sure the terms can be put into effect if the ex-spouse fails to perform.) With this provision in her decree, it was very simple for Sarah to go into court, tell a judge the facts, and get a "judge's deed" transferring the title to the house to her.

A self-executing provision also can be helpful when one party has agreed to take a monetary settlement in installments because the other party is short on cash. Let's say that Ella's ex-husband owns an apartment building. Their decree provides that if he sells the building (or another asset, such as his business or some shares of stock) before paying off the property settlement, or if he defaults on a payment for more than 30 days, the entire amount immediately comes due. That way, he can't just sell his assets, pocket the money, and take off without giving his ex-wife her share. (The same principle could apply if he withdrew money from a pension fund in which she had an interest—a topic we'll discuss later in this chapter.)

Delayed Sale of a Home

Frequently, because of young children and/or low interest on an existing mortgage, it seems wise to postpone sale of the marital home and division of the proceeds. If a woman has custody of the children, as is usually the case, the man may agree to let her live in the house until the youngest child reaches age 18. But self-executing provisions in the decree may, under certain conditions, trigger an earlier sale of the house or force an immediate payout of the man's interest in it. This might occur, for example, if the woman remarries, takes a live-in lover, or fails to maintain the house or to keep up the mortgage payments. Under the latter conditions, I've been able to obtain the right for the man to make repairs or make the delinquent mortgage payments so as to protect his stake.

Sometimes a court is called upon to enforce the spirit, rather than the letter of an agreement. In one case I handled recently, a woman we'll call Sheila was awarded possession of the family home, along with custody of the children, until her remarriage or until the youngest child reached 18. A year after the decree was entered, Sheila took a live-in lover.

The judge held that such an arrangement was contrary to the intent of the agreement between Sheila and her ex (my client), who had promised to provide shelter for her and their children but not for some other man. The judge therefore ordered immediate sale of the house—a step he held to have been triggered by Sheila's actions. In interpreting the terms of the agreement, the judge reasoned that even though this particular circumstance hadn't been specifically addressed in the decree, if the parties had foreseen it, they would have handled it that way. A similar situation might have arisen if Sheila had decided to move out of the house and put it up for rent, pocketing the income while her ex had to wait for his share until their youngest child turned 18.

Of course, my client wouldn't have had to go through such a complicated lawsuit if his original lawyer had foreseen that Sheila might take a live-in lover into the home she had been given the temporary right to occupy.

Unforeseen Circumstances Can Make Your Settlement Worthless

You may think you got a great deal on the property settlement, but if your ex files for bankruptcy, you may wind up with nothing. That's because, unlike alimony, obligations under a property settlement can be discharged if the person owing them is legally declared insolvent.

In her divorce agreement, Margery waived alimony in return for a property settlement of $150,000. But her ex, Dan, had just sunk most of his ready cash into a $300,000 commercial building in which he was opening a manufacturer's outlet for women's fashions. Margery agreed to wait three years to receive her money; she figured that Dan's business would prosper and he'd be good for it. But not trusting to chance, she also got him to secure the obligation by giving her a half-interest in the building. If she didn't get her $150,000 within three years, the building was to be sold and the proceeds to be split between them. Either way, she figured she was safe.

Unfortunately, women's hemlines dropped precipitously that year, and so did Dan's business. He was stuck with a large inventory of miniskirts that he couldn't even give away, as well as a stack of unpaid bills. In addition, what Dan hadn't told Margery or her lawyer at the time of the divorce was that he was already deeply in debt. With his business reversal, he soon owed half a million dollars and had to file for bankruptcy. Because his name was still on the title of the building (his sole asset) as sole owner, Margery's claim on it was no better than those of his other creditors and was discharged in bankruptcy along with the rest.

Margery would have been better advised not to have waived alimony. If she had reserved that question, she could have brought it up when Dan failed to make good on the property settlement. But she wasn't completely out of luck. Her lawyer was able to nullify the divorce agreement by showing that she had waived maintenance based on Dan's fraudulent concealment of his debts.

Another way Margery might have lost out is if Dan had died before making good on her cash settlement. In that case, other claims on his estate might have wiped out the asset she figured would be hers. An inexpensive and obvious way in which she could have protected herself from this risk would have been to take out term insurance on her ex's life in the amount of his $150,000 obligation to her.

Keep an Eye on Your Ex's Business

In another case, an ex-wife got a share not just in a tangible business asset like a building but in the business itself.

Because Jean's ex-husband was short on cash, as part of the property settlement she was awarded 20 percent of the stock in his small solely-owned manufacturing business. The agreement also included an option for him to buy her out by mutual agreement.

As a minority shareholder, Jean obviously didn't have much clout in the running of the business. Nevertheless, she wanted to keep an eye on her holdings—if for no other reason than to be able to gauge the optimal time to sell out to her ex. So she had her lawyer and her accountant keep tabs on the company. They found that her ex, rather than declaring dividends to the stockholders (that is, to Jean), was paying himself extra salary. Her lawyer filed a minority stockholder's suit on her behalf.

The moral of this story is that it's best not to settle for a share of a closely-held business you don't have a say in running. But if that's what your agreement provides, be prepared to hire competent legal and financial advisers.

Securing Your Insurance Benefits

Life insurance benefits are included under many settlement agreements; but here again, the insured (that is, your ex) may or may not follow through. You should get copies of the cancelled checks for each year's premium payments to verify that the policy is still in effect. In addition, write to the insurance company to inform them that you are the irrevocable beneficiary, enclosing a copy of your decree, and ask to be notified of any changes that are made in the policy. Otherwise, if your ex decides to take you off the policy (and perhaps substitute his or her new spouse), you may have to look to a court to enforce your claim.

Since most married couples carry group health insurance through the company for which one spouse works, one of the important considerations in a divorce is how the other party can get coverage. Some company plans provide conversion privileges without requiring the ex-spouse to take a medical examination as proof of insurability. However, conversion policies generally offer reduced benefits at substantially higher cost. Also, the former spouse is frequently not notified directly of the opportunity to elect coverage, which may be mentioned only on the insurance policy itself. Even if actual notice is given, the ex may have a very short time in which to apply for the conversion policy and pay the premium.

All this is changed under new federal legislation called COBRA (Consolidated Omnibus Budget Reconciliation Act of 1985). Under COBRA, most employers sponsoring group health plans must offer an employee's divorced or legally separated spouse and their children the opportunity to continue coverage at group rates, for periods varying up to three years. At the end of that time, an individual conversion health plan must be made available. However, if the ex-spouse becomes covered under another employer's group health plan or becomes entitled to Medicare, or if he or she remarries and is covered under the new spouse's group health plan, COBRA coverage ends.

If you become divorced or legally separated, it's essential to make sure the administrator of your health plan is promptly notified of that fact. You will in turn be notified of your right to choose continuation coverage.

Because this is a highly technical piece of legislation with detailed supporting regulations, I advise you to check with the plan administrator and/or seek legal advice regarding the specific requirements of your plan and of the act. Small firms and others exempt from COBRA may be covered by similar state legislation. At least 23 states had such laws as of 1987—the one in Illinois, for example, is the Spousal Health Insurance Rights Act, or SHIRA.

Securing Your Pension Rights

Inclusion of pension rights in property settlements has come about as a result of recognition of marriage as an economic partnership. Such intangible work-related assets as pension and retirement benefits are viewed as co-owned property, the fruit of both partners' contributions to the marriage venture.

With more than 10.2 million U.S. family households headed by women with a median income of only $14,200, pension coverage is vital. But until recently, it wasn't possible to divide up pension and profit-sharing plans at the time of a divorce without creating horrendous tax consequences. If a 50-year-old man had a $100,000 pension plan from which he was not entitled to withdraw money until age 65, how could the current value of his future benefits be determined? And even if it could be, how could he be expected to give his ex-wife a share, since he hadn't yet received it himself? Indeed, federal tax laws prohibited any assignment or diversion of an employee's accrued benefits to someone other than the plan participant.

Enter the Qualified Domestic Relations Order, better known as QUADRO. This new legal mechanism carves out an exception to the above rule for pension benefits awarded as part of a marital property settlement, child support, or alimony under a state's domestic relations law. With a QUADRO, part or all of one ex-spouse's IRA, Keough, or company or union pension plan can be given to the other ex-spouse with no unfavorable tax consequences and without cashing in the plan's assets prematurely, as long as the amount and form of benefits payable under the plan aren't changed. QUADROs are especially valuable for women who have not accumulated significant pension benefits themselves.

The QUADRO exception went into effect as of January 1, 1985. Pension plan administrators must honor a qualified order (decree or judgment) under which benefits were being paid as of that date, and administrators may also honor other orders entered before then.

This revolutionary new device offers opportunities for creative problem-solving after a decree has been entered. For example, I had a case in which the ex-wife had been awarded permanent alimony, but the ex-husband became disabled and could no longer afford to pay it. So we traded the alimony for half of his pension rights.

One caution: each plan is required to develop its own procedure dictating the steps to be taken, and that procedure must be followed to the letter. Another caution: as with an interest in your ex's business, an interest in his or her pension benefits may not be worth much without some control over the way the plan's assets are invested. Imprudent investments can eat up the funds you're counting on for your retirement. You don't want a high roller playing games with your money. If you can't get a share in investment decisions, see whether it's possible to spin off your share of the assets and handle the investments yourself.

Read Your Decree or Agreement

Knowledge is power. As you can see from the many examples in this chapter, to make sure you get what's coming to you, you must be familiar with the provisions of your divorce decree, property settlement, or live-in agreement. Review the document periodically, particularly if there's ongoing financial involvement with your ex. Also, be sure to check your decree or agreement if there's a significant change in your circumstances or your ex's.

By reading the document, you may be pleasantly surprised to find some favorable clauses, such as the self-executing provisions described at the beginning of this chapter, which will help you protect your hard-won benefits. Or the absence of certain types of provisions may leave the door open for you to obtain a better deal than you did originally, as I'll explain in part 3.

5

COLLECTING ALIMONY AND CHILD SUPPORT

A Florida man who owns four auto body shops and makes as much as $3,000 a week vows he'll go to jail before he'll pay the nearly $100,000 he owes in child support. His ex-wife, back in Chicago, struggles to support their four children on her $1,200-a-month salary as a word processor operator.

Another deadbeat father, who drives a Mercedes, tells his children he's sorry he hasn't been in touch with them, but he's been on a boat in Tahiti. A third man has never paid a penny to his five daughters. He picks up work as a handyman and takes his pay in cash to avoid being located.

If your ex-spouse makes more money than you do, and/or if you have custody of the children, your divorce decree or agreement may well provide for child support, alimony (spousal maintenance), or a combination of the two. If you're an unwed parent, you may be awarded child support if you can prove who the other parent is. But whether you actually receive all the money you're supposed to get is another question. In fact, the chances are more than 50-50 that you won't.

This country's child support system has justly been called "a national disgrace." Millions of single parents struggle with the financial hardship and emotional anguish of raising children with little or no support—support to which they are legally entitled. Most of those struggling single parents are women.

One Woman's Complaint

"Divorced women are the nation's 'new poor,'" an Indiana woman wrote to Ann Landers's syndicated advice column in August 1986.

This woman worked to put her ex-husband through a Ph.D. program, repaid his student loans, and moved with him from job to job across the country. Now he earns three times what she does, and she must take care of herself and their two children on $12,500 a year including child support.

Yet, as this mother admitted, she is "one of the lucky ones. Some women have NO child support because their husbands run from one state to another and nobody can catch them. Please don't suggest taking the bums to court. The cases are backed up for two years in our state."

This woman's story is all too typical. But the situation for her and the other mothers she described isn't necessarily as dark as she painted it, and action is being taken to brighten it. In chapter 10, I'll explain how you can seek an increase in your award if you believe it's inadequate. In this chapter, I'll tell you what steps you can take to enforce your award so you actually get the money that's due you.

For convenience, I'll use masculine pronouns to refer to the parent obligated to pay support and feminine pronouns to refer to the parent entitled to receive it. Even though nowadays an ex of either sex may be required to pay spousal maintenance or child support, it's still the woman who, nine times out of ten, has custody of the children. And, in 95 percent of cases of failure to pay child support, it's a man who's shirking his obligations.

The Economic Plight of Female-Headed Families

Theoretically, alimony and child support are supposed to make up for the income lost as a result of the departure of the chief breadwinner. In reality, though, the payments are generally too small and too sporadic to take up much of the slack. Indeed, according to a Colorado study, two-thirds of men ordered to make support payments are assessed amounts that are less than their car payments.

A 14-year study by the University of Michigan's Institute for Social Research found that men's standard of living rises in the year following a divorce because they are allocating a smaller proportion of their income to the support of their families. According to one estimate, the average support payment is only 13 percent of the man's income. Meanwhile, women's and children's living standards fall to 70 percent of their former level—even taking into account the women's increased earnings from employment. What's more, this situation is not usually transitory. Five years after a divorce, unless a woman has remarried—and only about half of divorced women wed again within that time—her economic position typically has not appreciably improved.

The economic plight of divorced, separated, and unwed mothers is a major factor in what has been called "the feminization of poverty." The loss of a man dumps many women and children out of the middle class. According to 1986 census data, the median income of female-headed families is only $14,200. Nearly one woman in three raising a family with an absent father—as compared with one in eighteen male-headed families—falls below the federal government's official poverty line. In 1988, based on the Consumer Price Index, this was a total money income of $11,650 (higher in Alaska and Hawaii) for a family of four.

An estimated one-fourth of all children born in the United States today will live at least part of their childhood and adolescence in poverty, and a child with an absent parent is four times more likely than a child in an intact family to be included in that group. About half of all children who live in households headed by women are on welfare, and payment of support is the biggest single factor in getting and keeping families off welfare. Thus the support of single mothers and their children is an urgent national priority.

Billions of Support Dollars Are Unpaid

More than $4 billion a year in court-ordered child support goes unpaid. According to a 1986 census survey, 61 percent of the 8.8 million women raising children with absent fathers have been awarded child support (about half of the others wanted it but couldn't get it). But fewer than half of the women with awards receive the full amount; the majority get part or nothing at all. In two-thirds of the cases, payments stop altogether within six years. And, of the 15 percent of divorced or legally separated women who have been awarded alimony, more than one-fourth get none of the money due them.

The average amount of alimony actually received in 1985 was about $3,700 a year. The average amount of child support actually received that year was only a little more than $2,200 (about $42 a week)—a 12.5 percent decrease in inflation-adjusted dollars from 1983. And the families most in need of the money—those below poverty level—got even less: an average of $1,380, or $26.50 a week. Meanwhile, the average man was making $1,000 more than two years before.

Why Don't They Pay?

Some men delinquent in their payments are unemployed or between jobs. But most of the worst offenders are not poor.

Some of them are angry and are determined not to pay. Some pay sporadically. Some withhold payments because they don't get to see the children; but some show no interest in seeing the children. Some leave town and lose touch with their former families, or purposely skip to avoid payments. Some are transferred out of state and eventually stop sending money. Divorced men who remarry (as three-fourths do within five years, according to the University of Michigan study) may prefer or feel more obligated to channel most of their resources to their new families. I know a man whose children of his second marriage go to expensive Ivy League schools, while the children of his first marriage take night classes at the local community college.

Not surprisingly, men generally pay more willingly when they have volunteered to do so (as occurs in approximately one-third of cases) than when a court has told them to. According to the census data, women with court-ordered payments receive only 56 percent of the amount due them, while women with voluntary agreements get 81 percent of what they are owed. The amount voluntarily agreed to tends to be higher, too, by approximately 13 percent.

Cracking Down on Deadbeat Dads

What can you do if you're not fortunate enough to have an ex ready and willing to pay for your upkeep and that of your children?

Some women find creative ways to loosen a man's wallet. For example, the ex-wife of the deadbeat who drives the Mercedes (whom I mentioned at the beginning of this chapter) managed to get hold of the automobile by paying a repair bill before her ex-husband did. Her ex couldn't get the car back until he paid her $2,500 in back child support.

If you're fed up with trying to get the man to pay up, you may be able to get him thrown into jail. In some instances, public prosecutors have obtained contempt citations and jail sentences to make examples of men who ducked their responsibilities. In a case originating in California, the U.S. Supreme Court recently upheld the jailing of child-support delinquents unless they can prove that they can't afford to make their court-ordered payments. Women's advocates hailed the ruling, saying that many deadbeats, faced with the threat of incarceration, "miraculously" find the money they claimed they didn't have.

Still, unless your ex has money stashed away somewhere, sending him to jail may provide hollow solace. A man behind bars, who isn't drawing paychecks, has less wherewithal to come up with your money. For that reason, some courts order deadbeat fathers jailed under work-release programs. In the California case I just referred to, the man didn't actually go to jail; his 25-day sentence was suspended, and he got three years' probation during which to catch up with his support payments.

Unfavorable publicity shames some men into paying up. When the Illinois Department of Public Aid in January 1988 posted a list of the state's "Ten Most Wanted" delinquent fathers, five of them coughed up $11,000. However, that was a mere drop in the bucket; the 10 owed nearly half a million dollars between them.

The Public Enforcement System

As I said, the federal and state governments are interested in enforcing support and maintenance orders not merely out of concern for women and children but because families without support are a drain on the welfare system.

In 1975 Congress established a federally-funded Child Support Enforcement Program, consisting of a network of state and local agencies to help welfare mothers collect delinquent payments. Congress also established a Federal Parent Locator Service to help women find absent fathers. But administration of the enforcement program was left to the states, with varying degrees of success. Reliance was mainly on noncoercive methods like monthly billings, voluntary wage assignments, telephone reminders, and delinquency notices. Women across the country have complained of getting the runaround, of watching their complaints crushed under pounds of paperwork, of waiting months or years for processing and then getting no results. Many men have been able to slip through the cracks simply by moving from one state to another.

Putting Teeth in Enforcement

Under the Federal Child Support Enforcement Amendments of 1984, states were required to strengthen and streamline their enforcement procedures. In a revolutionary move, states must adopt automatic collection of overdue child support for both welfare and nonwelfare parents.

What that means is that delinquent payments may now be deducted directly from an absent parent's paychecks, federal and state income tax refunds, unemployment or disability benefits, lottery winnings, profit-sharing plans, or other assets. Court-ordered alimony for a parent entitled to child support can be collected in the same way.

Wage withholding is triggered when payments are 30 days late. But a parent can request withholding even if payments are not delinquent. And states may choose—as Illinois has recently done—to have withholding take effect automatically from the start unless the parents and the judge agree to the contrary. Illinois Public Aid officials predict that this change alone will produce an additional $30 million a year and will prevent thousands of mothers from having to go on welfare while waiting for wage deductions to begin.

The Family Support Act of 1988 established automatic withholding from Day One nationwide. This provision is effective immediately for welfare cases, and in January 1994 it will be effective for new nonwelfare cases.

How Does Automatic Wage Withholding Operate?

Automatic wage withholding works like deductions for taxes and Social Security. The employer must deduct the support money directly from the employee's paycheck. In Illinois, for example, the amount deducted may be as little as 10 percent or as much as 60 percent of the paycheck, and penalties may be added for late payments.

A support obligation takes precedence over any other claim against wages, such as for payment of a past-due car loan or credit card bill. Computers keep track of the payments, and information on past-due support may be disclosed to credit companies.

Employers can't fire or discipline an employee because of support withholding. Employers may charge a small service fee for handling the paperwork; if they refuse to do the paperwork, they themselves become liable for the debt.

Other Enforcement Tools

In addition to wage withholding and interception of income tax refunds, a court may place a lien on a noncustodial parent's house, car, boat, or other property to cover unpaid support, or may put the property up for sale or in trust. A delinquent parent may be required to post bond to guarantee support, and, in some states, can be ordered to buy life insurance to cover alimony and child support in the event of his death. If unemployed, he may be ordered to get training or counseling and seek work.

Under the 1984 act, to help unwed mothers get child support, states must permit establishment of paternity for all children until at least the age of 18. This provision, which I discussed more fully in chapter 2, superceded the old short-term statutes of limitations. And while state paternity laws vary, courts may require the father, once identified, to pay not only for the child's future support but for past care as well. In some states, such as Kentucky, a paternity suit can be brought not only by the mother or the child but by any person or agency contributing to the child's support.

If Your Ex Disappears

What can you do if your ex tries to avoid his obligations by going underground or moving out of state? If you can't afford a private detective, you can try to track him down through state and federal locator services, which can tap into the resources of a variety of public agencies from the state motor vehicle division to the Internal Revenue Service.

The search may start with a review of automobile registrations, driver's license records, police and court records, and unemployment files. If your state locator service turns up a blank and you have reason to believe your ex is in another state, a request may be made to that state's locator service and/or to the Federal Parent Locator Service (FPLS).

The FPLS was overhauled in 1986 to handle more cases faster and more flexibly, at lower cost. In that year alone, the computerized service came up with addresses of absent parents in about 85 percent of the nearly one million requests submitted.

The FPLS, which also comes into play in cases of parental kidnapping, can trace an absent parent's whereabouts through his Social Security number and also may be able to obtain information about the location and extent of his assets.

If you don't have your ex's Social Security number, check old tax returns, hospital records, bank accounts, insurance policies, and other documents. If you still can't find it, don't despair; the FPLS may be able to dig up the number if you know your ex's birthplace and date and his parents' names.

Enforcement Across State Lines

Finding your ex is one thing; extracting payment is another. In one case I know of, a New York career woman had to drag her children to Florida for a child support action against her ex in Palm Beach. Normally, though, such a trip shouldn't be necessary. You should be able to collect from your ex even if he has moved thousands of miles away (provided, of course, that he's working), without having to pursue him yourself or hire an out-of-state lawyer.

All states have some version of the Uniform Reciprocal Enforcement of Support Act (URESA), which enables them to cooperate with each other in bringing fugitives to justice. Under URESA, a court in one state or jurisdiction can enforce an order obtained in a court in another state or jurisdiction. Instead of chasing your ex to wherever he lives, all you have to do is file a petition in your home state, which is then forwarded (free of charge) to a court in your ex's state. Payments are made to a clerk of the court, and scofflaws can be criminally prosecuted.

URESA is not foolproof. The provisions in one state may not be compatible with those of another. And delays are common in interstate cases. Even after your ex is located and served with notice of the enforcement action, it may take a long time to get a court date. Meanwhile, he may move again.

The 1984 federally-mandated reforms eventually are expected to promote uniform procedures among states. Many of the enforcement techniques apply across state lines, and the states are given financial incentives to use them.

Box 3

How To Get Help from a Public Agency

To get help from the public enforcement system, contact your city, county, or state child support enforcement agency. If you're not on public assistance, you may have to pay a fee of up to $25—far less than it would cost to hire a private attorney. (Welfare parents receive agency assistance automatically, without charge.) A caseworker will be assigned to steer your case through the system. In some states, costs for locating an absent parent and working with agencies in other states may be deducted from your support payments. Your caseworker should be able to estimate how much the deduction would amount to in your case.

First you need a court support order or (in a few states) another type of legally binding agreement; if you don't have one, the agency can help you get one. It will help if you've kept careful records of the payments your ex has made and missed and of property he owns; the latter may be attached for unpaid support.

Even if your support isn't in arrears, you can ask the state enforcement agency to collect it for you. If your support order was issued or modified before October 1, 1985, you must specifically request wage withholding—it won't kick in automatically unless your judgment contains a withholding order.

The Office of Child Support Enforcement of the U.S. Department of Health and Human Services publishes a *Handbook on Child Support Enforcement*, a valuable how-to guide, which answers many commonly-asked questions. For a free copy, write to Handbook, Department 628M, Consumer Information Center, Pueblo, CO 81009.

Normally under URESA you'll end up with monthly install-ment payments rather than a lump sum settlement. If the amount of delinquent support is relatively small and/or you can't afford legal fees, URESA is probably the way to go. If, however, there's a lot of money involved, it may be worthwhile to hire a lawyer.

In one case I handled, a man had disappeared for 10 years and was more than $30,000 in arrears when one of his grown children, who needed money for college, heard that he was living in Texas, had remarried, had a good job, and owned some real estate. I obtained a judgment against the man in Illinois and then went to Texas and asked the court there to recognize it, which the court did. The judgment was for the amount owed plus interest, which, when compounded, came to a total of more than $60,000. Since the man couldn't come up with that much cash, I instituted collection proceedings, placed a lien on his property, and forced the sale of some of it.

How Well Are the Reforms Working?

Although some states have been slow to implement the 1984 federal reforms, some improvement is evident. During the 1986 fiscal year, $3.2 billion was collected nationwide—a 20 percent increase since 1985 and an 83 percent increase since 1982. Also, between 1982 and 1986, 40 percent more unwed fathers were identified and their support obligations established, and 34 per-cent more absent parents were located. In Cook County, Illinois, in the first nine months that automatic wage withholding was in effect, some 1,500 families were able to recover back child sup-port without going to court.

Of course, as with any computerized system, there are in-evitable bugs, and innocent people who can get hurt. I've heard horror stories about men who were arrested for nonpayment just because of a computer error. And, despite the safeguards against loss of a job because of wage withholding, an irritated employer may be able to find some other excuse to fire the man—thus, in effect, killing the goose that laid the golden egg.

Another problem in dealing with a computer is that there's no room for flexibility or cooperation. What if an order of withholding has been entered and a father wants to buy his son a new snowsuit instead of making his normal payment? What if a woman who has custody wants to go away for a couple of months and leave the children with her ex and is willing to have him suspend support payments during that time? Such informal adjustments become difficult when a computer is in charge.

Although these enforcement procedures were set up to avoid the need for legal representation, the system is still far from perfect. You may find your case getting lost in the shuffle or tied up in red tape. Courts are frequently backlogged, and what would seem to be a simple proceeding may take a year or more. It's up to you to decide whether your situation warrants the expense of hiring a lawyer.

If you do deal with the public agencies on your own, be assertive but not pushy. Ask questions, make suggestions to your caseworker, take notes, and keep records of everything pertaining to your case. Follow up politely to see what progress is being made. Be businesslike and unemotional. If you're not satisfied with what's being done, you can appeal (preferably in writing) to the head of your county's child support enforcement office or to the director of the state agency.

What If Your Ex is Unemployed or Self-Employed?

While an order of withholding may be effective against a man who's employed, more often than not the deadbeats are men who are self-employed, unemployed, or between jobs, not those who work for steady wages. For example, if your ex is self-employed, it may be fairly simple for him to avoid withholding by suspending his salary and taking his money in the form of profit distributions.

Although public prosecutors will take such cases, they tend to be more complex and therefore to warrant private representation. A private attorney will probably be more interested in such a case and, since you'll be paying for his or her services, is likely to give it more immediate and sustained attention and to come up with more creative approaches to put pressure on your ex. If you depend on the public prosecutor, you may have to wait months or years for action. You can't just pick up the phone, as you would with your own lawyer, and say, "Hey, what's going on with my case?" The prosecutor assigned to the case may spend a couple of months on it and then get transferred to another division, and you'll have to start from scratch with someone else.

If your ex is temporarily out of work, it's smart to wait until he gets a job before initiating enforcement action. A woman named Jane came to me and said that her ex-husband, Jim, had lost his job and was three weeks behind in his payments. She wanted to take him to court right away. I talked her out of it. If we had gone into court immediately, what would have been the most likely result? The judge probably would have either (1) let Jim off the hook for a while by abating his support obligation until he could find employment, or (2) reduced his support obligation because of his worsened circumstances. By forcing Jim's hand, we would have pushed him into seeing a lawyer who would have explained these options to him—options of which he might otherwise have been unaware. But because we waited to file an enforcement action until Jim was working again, it was too late for him to pursue those options, and we were able to recover all of the back payments he had missed while unemployed.

Pros and Cons of Court-Processed Payments

Your state may provide an option for payment of court-awarded moneys through an official such as the clerk of the court. This is not the same as automatic wage withholding; just because you have your payments collected through the court doesn't mean that you will automatically get your money. It's up to your ex to send it in. However, in some states (such as Idaho, Illinois, and North Dakota), the public prosecutor will enforce compliance.

Are you better off having your ex send the payments directly to you or through the court? That depends chiefly on how well you get along with your ex.

If the two of you are on good terms, there are definite pluses to dealing directly with each other. For one thing, you avoid red tape. I've heard of cases in which it took as long as six weeks from the time the noncustodial parent wrote a check to the clerk of the court until the day the custodial spouse got the money. If you believe you can count on your ex to pay you promptly, why not keep things friendly and avoid delay?

Then, too, as I've mentioned, computers are notoriously rigid. When you're dealing directly with your ex, you both may find it convenient to make occasional special arrangements: "This month, instead of giving me my $500, why don't you just pay Karen's tuition at summer camp?" or, "Since you're out of a job right now, I'll give you a pass on the support payments for a couple of months." You can make such "deals" more easily if you don't have a court looking over your shoulder.

I prefer to start out by giving a man the benefit of the doubt by assuming that he's going to meet his obligations. If not, we can most likely petition for enforcement after the divorce and insist on a court order that future payments are to be made through the clerk of the court.

Defending Against Enforcement Actions

Here I must put in a word to the men, or whoever is paying support: if you cut your own deal, don't rely on a verbal agreement. A frequent defense against enforcement actions is, "She said I didn't have to pay that much." And it may be true. But if you didn't get it in writing, you probably don't have a leg to stand on.

Ralph agreed to pay Ellen $800 a month in unallocated alimony and child support, and that amount was written into the award. He later realized that he had overextended himself and could afford only half that much. "Don't worry, I'll give you a break," Ellen told him. "Just pay me $400 a month." Ralph dutifully paid that amount for the next 10 years. The next year she changed her mind and slapped him with a suit for the arrearage plus interest, claiming that she never had agreed to the reduction. He was stuck. It was his word against the written document.

It's not too difficult to get a court order suspending support payments because of some temporary circumstance, such as a strike or layoff that cuts off your income for the time being. Taking that precaution can forestall enforcement problems. And if you're making a permanent alteration in your arrangement, as Ralph and Ellen did, it definitely should be reduced to writing.

Another piece of advice: save all receipts and records, and pay by check whenever possible. Many times a father will buy his daughter a new dress, or pay the dentist bill, instead of his regular support payment. Six years later, his ex may suddenly charge that his support is in arrears.

I represented a man whose ex-wife claimed he owed her $18,000 in alimony. He insisted he had paid her in cash, though he had no receipts to prove it. (Judges hear that excuse every day—it's like "The check is in the mail.") My client learned his lesson the hard way: although he was able to trace part of the money, he wound up having to pay most of it a second time.

Tactics in Enforcement Cases

Women need to be on the lookout for certain tactics that men and their lawyers sometimes use in enforcement cases. One is to threaten a counterclaim for change of custody to get a woman to back off from a legitimate claim for support. A woman can be caught in a bind if that happens, especially if she's not represented by a lawyer. Since many state enforcement agencies provide no representation in custody disputes, the mother may risk losing her child if she or the state pursues the support claim. And if she's on welfare, she may have no choice in the matter: the state may pursue the claim whether she wants to or not.

Some states, like Alaska, have dealt with this problem by forbidding the raising of issues of custody and visitation in support enforcement cases. As automatic wage withholding takes hold, the use of this particular tactic may diminish.

Don't Give Up

My last words to those of you who are trying to collect your court-ordered alimony and child support are, don't get discouraged and don't give up. Courts and legislatures are working to make these obligations truly enforceable. This chapter may have made you aware of avenues you hadn't known existed. If one avenue doesn't work, try another. If you persevere, your efforts are likely to be rewarded.

6

ENFORCING
VISITATION RIGHTS

More than half of the children of divorce see the absent parent (usually the father) less than once a month, and one-third never see him. Children of unwed parents are even less likely ever to see their fathers. That information comes from a census study, which found that the longer parents are apart, the more likely it is that children will lose contact with the noncustodial parent—especially if the mother has custody and has remarried. What isn't clear is, who's responsible for this lack of contact?

Do Moms Keep Dads and Kids Apart?

FAIR (Father's Advocacy, Information and Referral), a nationwide fathers' organization, claims that more than 77 percent of 2,228 fathers the group surveyed are unable to see their children because of "divorce warfare" and an alleged failure of courts to protect visitation rights. Especially during holidays, fathers who are denied access to their children run the risk of becoming depressed and subject to accidents, alcohol and drug abuse, illness, and suicide.

The fathers' advocates complain that much is done to help mothers collect child support, but not much is done to make them honor visitation rights. Although free counsel and assistance are available for child support enforcement, in most places there's no similar service for fathers who aren't being permitted to see their children.

Other studies suggest that it's fathers who tend to stay away from their former families, while mothers wish that Dad would spend more time with the kids. Geoffrey Grief, author of *Single Fathers*, found this attitude among 65 percent of the mothers he surveyed, while only 7 percent felt the father was overly involved with the children. These findings are consistent with my experience: most women want their children's father to devote time to them.

How Common Are Visitation Complaints?

It's difficult to get a handle on the true extent of visitation problems. One approach might be to compare the numbers of visitation complaints with those filed in support cases. The Domestic Relations Office of Travis County, Texas, reported only 746 complaints about denial of visitation in 1983, as compared with 13,808 complaints of failure to pay child support—more than 18 times as many. But we don't know how many visitation problems occurred without complaints being filed. It seems far more likely that a person would take legal action to recover money essential to a family's livelihood than to enforce visitation.

No matter how frequent or infrequent denial of visitation may be, it's no less disturbing when it does occur. Parent and child both lose out when deprived of contact with each other. The purpose of this chapter, then, will be to tell you how to enforce your visitation rights when your ex appears to be interfering with them. For simplicity's sake, I'll be addressing the father, but what I have to say will, of course, apply to noncustodial mothers as well.

What's Behind Visitation Problems?

As I said, most women welcome a showing of paternal responsibility. So, if a man is having trouble getting to see his children, I'd suspect there's something unusual going on. For example, there may be extraordinary hostility between him and the mother. She may have psychological problems. She may be neglecting or abusing the children and trying to hide that fact. (More on that point toward the end of this chapter.)

Sometimes there's a new man in the house who forcibly objects to the ex-husband's coming around, and the woman may not be able to control him. One father, who had been beaten up by his ex-wife's lover, came to me for help. I filed for an injunction against the woman and her lover forbidding them to interfere with my client's visitation rights. It turned out that the woman's boyfriend was on drugs, so we filed for custody. At that point she was faced with a stark choice: give up her lover or give up her child. She chose her child, and my client got his visitation.

Child Support and Visitation: The Chicken and the Egg

Visitation problems sometimes are linked with support issues. Does a man withhold support because he's not allowed to see his children, or does the woman refuse visitation because her support checks come late—or not at all? This strikes me as a chicken-or-egg question. What ordinarily happens is that each party believes himself or herself to be "getting even" for the other's wrongful behavior. Often it's virtually impossible to determine who was originally at fault.

It does seem likely that a man who isn't paying child support or is behind in his payments isn't seeing his children very often. But he may be purposely staying out of sight to avoid arguments about child support or because he's afraid that his ex will go after him for her money. Indeed, in a 1984 study, when North Carolina fathers involved in child support enforcement actions were asked whether they had experienced any significant difficulties with getting visitation, only 8 percent of the welfare fathers and 13 percent of nonwelfare fathers said yes.

Withholding Support Can Be Hazardous To Your Financial Health

Men who do withhold support in retaliation for denial of their visitation rights are playing a dangerous game, as a Chicago man found out. At first, everything went smoothly after his divorce: he paid his ex-wife $300 a month and got to see his son and daughter every other weekend. But then he and his ex began to quarrel over his objections to her lifestyle. He complained that the house was filthy and noisy. She told him to mind his own business and began talking against him to the children. The next few times he came to pick them up, he found that their mother had made other plans for them. Finally he stopped paying child support and tried to get custody.

Nine months and hundreds of dollars in attorneys' fees later, the court turned down the custody change and ordered automatic wage withholding of all the back child support. His visitation rights? A separate question, the court said.

Although some states do make visitation and child support awards interdependent, in most places denial of visitation is not a legal ground for refusal to pay child support. And, by the same token, nonpayment of child support isn't normally a valid ground for denying visitation. The two are usually considered to be independent obligations and should be dealt with separately. The custodial parent should allow visitation while at the same time taking action to collect delinquent support. And the noncustodial parent should make the required support payments while at the same time taking action to enforce visitation rights.

There are exceptions. For example, a California appellate court held that a mother's "outrageous" efforts to alienate a child from his father may relieve him of his support obligation. And the Tennessee Supreme Court ruled that a noncustodial father need not pay child support during a period in which the mother fled the state to deprive the father of court-ordered visitation.

Under most circumstances, however, I don't recommend cutting off child support as a weapon to enforce visitation rights. Taking the law into your own hands is risky—and usually unnecessary. In my experience, when a man wants to see his children, courts are ready and willing to help him do it without depriving them of needed support. In fact, assuming he knows where his children are, it's a lot easier for a man to make his ex let him see them than it is for her to force him to pay child support. He may be able to plead poverty, but she has no valid basis for denying visitation unless she can prove that contact with the father would be harmful to the child.

Visitation Rights of Unwed Fathers

Unwed fathers, unlike divorced fathers, traditionally have been expected to pay child support without having contact with their children. But this situation is changing. More and more, courts are holding that an unwed father has the right to see his child. So, if a woman files a paternity suit, she should realize that the man is probably going to get visitation.

As I mentioned in chapter 2, we're also seeing more reverse paternity suits brought by fathers who want to play a role in their children's lives—not necessarily to obtain custody but to have contact with their children. These fathers say, "I don't mind paying child support; I want to see that kid." But often the mother says, "I don't want your money and I don't want you to have anything to do with the child." Fathers in such situations are taking steps to enforce their rights.

In one extreme case, when the mother refused to let the father see the child, he snatched the youngster. The action wasn't technically a violation of any law or court order, because she had never obtained custody. The woman had to seek custody in order to get her child back, and part of the court order was a grant of visitation rights to the father.

In most cases, an unwed father won't have to take such drastic measures to secure visitation rights. Nor need he wait for the mother to initiate a paternity suit; he can file one himself, requesting visitation rights once he has established that he's the child's father.

So, virtually everything I'm about to say about enforcing visitation applies to unwed as well as to divorced parents, except that an unwed father often will get less visitation time. In many cases, there has not been an ongoing relationship with the mother (it may even have been a one-night stand) or with the child (the father may suddenly emerge out of the blue and want to enter the child's life). The mother may have married, and the child may have established a psychological link with the stepfather. A court may be reluctant to disturb that relationship in order to afford full visitation rights to the biological father.

Legal Tools for Enforcing Visitation

If your exercise of your visitation rights is being hindered or blocked, you can petition a court to enforce the decree or order that gave you those rights. Visitation rights are enforceable under the Uniform Child Custody Jurisdiction Act, which has been enacted in some form in all 50 states, the District of Columbia, and the Virgin Islands; and under the federal Parental Kidnapping Prevention Act of 1980. In addition, criminal parental kidnapping laws in some states cover interference with visitation rights.

There are several simple but effective steps that can be taken. If your custody order doesn't require your ex to keep you informed of where you can reach your child, you can ask the court to add such a provision. You can also ask for a requirement that your ex get the court's permission before moving your child out of state. (More on that in chapter 10.) If your ex is constantly interfering with visitation, you might ask the court to order her to post bond to ensure that future visits will take place unimpeded.

You may be able to sue and collect money damages for denial of visitation rights. In one 1985 case, a father got $40,000 in compensatory damages and $10,000 in punitive damages. The very filing of such a suit may be enough to make your ex come around.

As part of the federal Family Support Act of 1988, Congress allocated $4 million for each of two years to strengthen the states' visitation enforcement. One purpose is to give noncustodial parents better access to information about their children.

Another is to establish procedures for expedited handling of visitation disputes.

Enforcing Specific Visitation

Your visitation award may provide for a specific amount or schedule of visitation time—say, Monday nights from 5:00 PM to 9:00 PM, Saturdays from 9:00 AM to 6:00 PM, and alternate Sundays. Or an order may simply call for "reasonable visitation," with the details to be worked out at the discretion of the parties. (Courts often provide for reasonable visitation when the parties are seemingly on good terms or when a man's working hours are irregular and won't accommodate a specified weekly schedule of visitation.)

If your visitation rights are precisely spelled out and your ex habitually fails to let you see your child when you're supposed to, it's a relatively simple matter to take care of. All you have to do is to establish that your ex didn't let you see the child on such-and-such occasions for no good reason, and a judge will order her to comply. If she doesn't, she can be held in contempt of court. You may request, and the judge may order, makeup days—extra visits to compensate for the ones you missed. Or the judge may take more drastic measures, from locking up your ex for a weekend to changing custody.

Note that I said the denial of visitation must be "habitual" and "for no good reason." An isolated incident probably won't cause a court to act. It's unrealistic to insist that your scheduled visitations take place like clockwork, regardless of what else is happening in your child's life. What if your daughter is sick? What if your son is invited to his best friend's birthday party, and it happens to be on your visitation day? If you're truly concerned about your child's best interests, you have to be somewhat flexible. Ask yourself whether it's possible that you're the one who is being unreasonable and that your ex may have had a valid reason for cancelling your visitation.

On the other hand, if your ex offers excuses—even apparently good ones—three times in a row, you have cause to suspect that she's playing games with you.

Documenting Visitation Denials

In case you should decide to go to court, the following tips will help you establish proof:

• Take someone along to witness your ex turning you down for visitation, so it's not just your word against hers. Knock on your ex's door at the time when you're supposed to be there. I've even had some men persuade police officers to go with them to document the visitation attempt.

• Keep a journal and fully describe each denial of visitation. You'll be able to refer to your journal in court to refresh your memory. If you've carefully logged the excuses your ex gave from one time to the next, it will become pretty obvious to the judge whether or not these were normal occurrences.

Of course, if you're going to take your ex to court, you'd better make sure your own hands are clean. One man filed a visitation complaint, and his ex-wife promptly filed a countersuit for back child support. The judge found them both in contempt. They spent the weekend in the same jail and haven't given each other a bit of trouble since!

Sometimes There's Good Reason for Denying Visitation

Actually, visitation cases seldom go to trial. Normally the woman's lawyer will say to her, "Look, I don't have any defense unless you can show that your child will be endangered by being left in your ex's charge." Likewise, the man's lawyer will advise him to examine his own behavior and make sure there's no reason he shouldn't have visitation: "You're not taking the kid to bars, or dropping him off with your girlfriend while you go to the track, are you?" Thus before the parties step into the courtroom, it'll probably be pretty clear who's at fault and what needs to be done.

If the mother feels that there's legitimate reason why the father shouldn't be seeing the child, she does have some recourse. Perhaps the father is recovering from a drug addiction or just got out of jail. The mother can ask to have his visitation rights suspended until he can prove that he has rehabilitated himself. Or a court may award supervised visitation, allowing the father to see the child only in the presence of another adult, such as a clergyman or social worker. This may be done if the judge concludes that the father can't be entrusted with responsibility for the child, or that the child might be subject to physical or psychological harm by seeing the father alone.

When Visitation Isn't Working, Try Mediation

When a mother resists visitation, it may be because the child and the father don't get along. The woman will tell the court, "It would be nice if my child would spend time with her father, but she doesn't want to. I can't make her." Legally speaking, there's no disputing the father's rights. But practically speaking, what's the mother to do? Her child is hysterical, holding onto the door and screaming, "I won't go with him!" Should a judge throw the woman in jail for refusing to surrender the child?

When the father-child relationship is rocky, or if the two haven't seen each other for a long time and visitation is to be resumed, court-ordered mediation may be the solution. Most progressive court systems today have some form of mediation or court-enforced counseling. Mediation works differently in different jurisdictions, but the basic concept is the same. Trained social workers talk with the child, the father, the mother, and other members of the household to try to get to the bottom of the problem. In some cases, the social worker may recommend therapy. Mediation also may be ordered if it appears that the father isn't really interested in seeing the child but is merely using his visitation rights as an excuse to come over and bother his ex. Professional intervention usually works fairly well. It gets people talking to each other and working toward a goal that's not a win-lose situation. And if it doesn't resolve the basic problem, at least it puts a band-aid on it for a while so that people will open up a line of communication and get some kind of relationship going.

Just as some women fail to pursue their potential remedies for collecting child support, some men are unaware of their options for resolving a visitation problem. A man will say, "I give up. I go over there and the kids don't want to see me. I pay my child support and that's the end of it." In such situations, court-ordered mediation may be the answer.

What Is "Reasonable Visitation"?

If your award provides for reasonable visitation, things are not as cut-and-dried as if a visitation schedule is clearly laid out. Who's to say what's reasonable and what's not? If you want to see your daughter on Thursday, and your ex says, "No, you just saw her on Tuesday," you can't just point to the decree and say, "This is my time." Your ex, for her part, may become upset if a planned two-week summer visit with you stretches into two months, but you may claim the long visit is reasonable because you and your child are getting along well and you haven't seen each other for quite a while.

However, flexibility doesn't mean anything goes. If you feel that you're not getting enough visitation time and can't get satisfaction from your ex, you can plead your case to a judge. Courts generally follow minimum guidelines for what constitutes reasonable visitation (see Box 4). If you're getting less than that, you have a very good chance of winning.

It used to be thought sufficient if a divorced father saw his children three or four times a year and a few weeks during the summer. But courts now recognize the importance of a father's influence. The aim is to give the father as much quality visiting time with his child as possible, without disrupting the child's life.

In deciding what's reasonable, courts take into consideration the child's age and schedule. An infant who's being breast-fed may not be able to be away from the mother overnight. The older a child gets, the more time the child's activities take up, and the more say the child should have about how much time to spend with the noncustodial parent. If a 17-year-old doesn't want to come to his father's house on Sunday or has made other plans, it's pretty hard to make him go there. Still, as long as the youngster is not legally emancipated, the court has jurisdiction to make decisions that affect his life.

Box 4

Guidelines for Reasonable Visitation

The following minimum guidelines are typical of those accepted by courts for children between the ages of about two and thirteen. If you have "reasonable visitation" rights, you should be able to see the child at least:

•Every other weekend and one night during the week.

•A week or two in summer.

•A week at spring break and Christmas break (alternate years).

•Father's Day.

•Other holidays (such as Memorial Day, Fourth of July, Labor Day, Thanksgiving, Christmas, and other religious holidays) on an alternating basis.

•The child's birthday (alternate years).

You can probably get just about any reasonable variation on the above. For example, if you don't have room to keep your child overnight, you might have dinner together after work twice a week. If you have joint custody, you may be able to get even more time. (Even with joint custody, one parent usually has primary physical custody of the child and the other has visitation rights.)

What To Say If She Says . . .

If you suspect your ex is making excuses to keep you away from your child—or even if her reasons are genuine—there are ways you can handle the situation short of going to court. Here are a couple of typical examples:

(1) *She*: Lucy's sick today. She can't go out with you.

He: What's wrong with her?

She: She has a bad cold.

He: No problem. We can do something indoors.

She: That won't work. She has a doctor's appointment this afternoon.

He: I'll take her. What time is the appointment, and where's the doctor's office?

Comment: If a two-year-old has a cold, that may be good reason to put off a visit with Dad; maybe not if it's a twelve-year-old. If this sort of thing becomes habitual, insist on talking to the doctor, rather than just accepting your ex's word.

(2) *She*: Tommy can't go with you. He has a Little League game this afternoon.

He: Fine—I'll take him. It'll be fun. We'll go out for a hamburger afterwards.

She: No, after the game he has to practice violin. His lesson is tomorrow.

He: OK, then we'll skip the hamburger. What time shall I pick him up for the game?

Comment: This one has many variations: "She has a ballet lesson" . . . "He's going to a birthday party" . . . "She's been invited to my parents' farm for the weekend," and so on. I've observed that some mothers (purposely or not) load up a child with activities so there's not much time left for Dad. Your ex needs to recognize that time spent with you is as important as, or more so than, a child's other pursuits. If you can't accompany your child to a scheduled activity, insist on a makeup visit. If the problem persists, some activities may have to be dropped.

Understand, though, that there are times when visitation really would be a burden on your child. If you're willing to bend on those occasions, your ex may be more accommodating at other times.

Custody: The Ultimate Remedy

If you've tried everything and your ex still insists on keeping you from seeing your child, you may want to consider seeking a change of custody. Courts have been known to order a custody change when there has been flagrant failure to honor visitation rights. Even if you didn't originally want custody, you may decide that you do if it's the only way you can get to see your child. You can hedge your bets by coupling a custody petition with a petition for visitation enforcement.

A custody change also may be your best remedy if your ex tries to move your child out of state without good cause. This in effect denies you your visitation rights—as I'll discuss in chapter 10.

When Emergency Action Is Called For

I generally don't advocate taking the law into your own hands. But there are times when that's exactly what a concerned, responsible parent must do. Picture this scenario:

Stanley hasn't seen his six-year-old son Max for some time. Every time he's tried, his ex, Diane, has some lame excuse. The last time he succeeded in seeing the boy, three months ago, Diane left a message to pick him up at her friend Sally's house, because she had to work. Stanley rang Sally's bell half a dozen times at 11:00 AM on a Saturday. She finally appeared at the door partially disrobed and heavily made up. When he explained that he was there to pick up his son, she shoved Max out the door. The boy looked pale and thin, his clothes were dirty, and when Stanley took him to a restaurant for lunch, he wolfed down everything in sight.

Stanley suspects that both Diane and Sally are prostitutes and that Max is being neglected or abused. But he lacks firm evidence. The only thing he's sure about is that his visitation rights are being obstructed.

Stanley has two choices: he can apply to a court to enforce visitation, which may involve some delay, or he can attempt to take possession of his child and go to court afterward.

In one case I handled, I advised a father to take the latter course. He picked up his son after school, and within 24 hours we had filed an emergency petition for a change of custody. Was the father guilty of kidnapping? No, because in Illinois and some other states, if a noncustodial parent who has reason to believe that a child has been abandoned, mistreated, abused, or threatened with such treatment takes the child and, within 72 hours, petitions for emergency relief, no crime has been committed.

Note that Stanley was first alerted to the situation because of problems with visitation. That's how these cases often develop; a custodial parent who isn't taking proper care of the child will try to hide that fact by preventing the other parent from seeing the child.

So, if your visitation is being interfered with (or even if it isn't) and you believe your child's health and safety are in danger, you may not have to wait; depending on the law in your state, you may be able to act to protect your child. Of course, you should consult a lawyer before taking such action.

Enforcement or Modification?

As you can see, there's not necessarily a clear-cut line between enforcing an order and modifying (changing or amending) it. To cite just two examples mentioned in this chapter and the last one, an attempt to enforce visitation rights may lead to a change of custody, and an attempt to collect back support may prompt an alteration in the level of support.

In part 3, we'll look at what you can do if you want to improve upon the existing situation created by your decree, order, or agreement.

PART III

Can You Get a Better Deal?

7

WHAT CAN AND CAN'T BE CHANGED AND HOW TO TELL THE DIFFERENCE

Up to now, we've been concerned with how to enforce the rights you already have. But what if you feel you didn't get a fair deal? What if things have changed, and a settlement that seemed equitable no longer does? What if arrangements that sounded workable aren't working out? Is there anything you can do? In many cases, yes.

What Is Modification?

To make sure we have our terms straight, let's briefly review the three main types of cases we're dealing with in this book. **Enforcement** cases, the kind I discussed in part 2, seek to carry out the terms of a decree, order, or agreement as written. **Modification** cases seek to change some of those terms, usually in response to changed circumstances. **Nullification** cases seek to invalidate, or throw out, the entire document.

Don't Try To Be Your Own Lawyer

The best way to find out whether or not you can get your decree, order, or agreement modified is to see an attorney. The facts and fine print are different in every case, and only a professional who looks closely at your situation can properly evaluate your chances. You should have a lawyer anyway if you want to petition the court for a modification.

Many times these cases don't go to trial, and sometimes nothing is even filed; the matter is simply negotiated between the two parties and their attorneys. But even if there's an out-of-court settlement, it's essential to put it in writing and get a judge to sign an order, to make sure the change is on record and to avoid future difficulties.

I have a case in which a man had to take a pay cut and persuaded his ex-wife to reduce his child support obligation from $500 to $250 a month. He made the mistake of relying on her word. Now, 10 years later, he's back in court with nothing in writing to support his story, and she's claiming he owes her $30,000 in back child support.

The purpose of this chapter isn't to enable you to be your own lawyer but to give you a general idea of the types of things that can and can't be changed. I'll lay out some broad legal principles now, and in succeeding chapters we'll look more closely at common types of modifications and I'll suggest tips and strategies.

When Is a Deal a Deal?

The issues in a divorce case generally fall into three categories: property division, arrangements for the children (custody, support, and visitation), and alimony (spousal maintenance). Similar issues are involved in the breakup of an unwed relationship.

As a general rule, anything having to do with children can be modified; anything having to do with division of property can't. If a woman got the furniture, she got the furniture; her ex can't later say, "I want to exclude the grandfather's clock, it belonged to my

Aunt Mary." If the man received his pension or his medical practice, clear of any financial interest on the woman's part, it's his. It's a dead issue—unless a creative lawyer can find an ambiguity in the wording or grounds for nullification, or the other party agrees to the change. On the other hand, even if a decree specifically designates a child support figure or visitation schedule as "nonmodifiable," a court will probably not enforce such a provision.

Let's look more closely, then, at modifications affecting children and the rationale behind them.

There's No Such Thing As Permanent Custody

If the court gave you "permanent custody," you may think you can relax and never have to worry again about your ex getting control of your child. Not true. Even though the words may say it, there's no such thing as permanent custody.

The term **permanent custody** is used to distinguish it from temporary custody, which may be granted while a case is still going on or before the judge has a chance to hear from one party. Custody becomes "permanent" when a final decree or order is entered. But that's another misnomer: just because an order is marked "final" doesn't mean it can't be changed later.

In fact, there's practically nothing permanent or final when it comes to the welfare of a child—and for good reason. A child isn't a possession, to be treated like a piece of furniture and traded off once and for all. (One judge I know doesn't even like to use the word custody because it implies possession.) The child wasn't a participant in the settlement between the parents, and his or her well-being can't be sacrificed for the sake of sticking to what they agreed to. The court is a protector of children. Anything a court would construe as affecting a child's best interests, such as a change in the circumstances of either parent—financial, marital, physical, psychological, emotional—can be grounds for modification, as I'll explain in detail in chapter 8.

A change of custody may be triggered by unjustified denial of visitation or by neglect or abuse of the child. A court may order a change of custody if the custodial parent has an unstable lifestyle or when it appears that the noncustodial parent now can make a better home for the child. Also, as I'll explain in chapter 9, joint custody can be changed to sole custody and vice versa, or it can be modified by giving the other parent residential custody.

Visitation Gets Modified All the Time

It's very difficult to live up to the letter of the law with regard to visitation. People get sick, schedules change, parents take vacations, children have their own activities. Parents constantly "modify" visitation by informal agreement. Even if there's a set schedule specified in the award, it's assumed that the parties will be reasonable enough to accept normal variances without running to court every time. If you're experiencing chronic problems, though, you can seek a formal modification.

Here's one place where careful draftsmanship of the original agreement can pay off. Suppose the two lawyers—taking their cue from the parties, who wanted to keep things on a friendly basis—drew up an agreement that provided simply for reasonable visitation. What was reasonable yesterday may not be reasonable today; and a parent who can't afford to go back to court for a modification may in effect wind up with no visitation rights whatsoever. For example, what if your ex decides that it's "unreasonable" for you to see your child because she doesn't approve of the woman you're dating? Rather than opening the door to such problems, I like to specify a fallback schedule in the original agreement (see Box 4, chapter 6), in case visitation becomes an issue.

Moving a child out of state involves a major modification of visitation rights; in chapter 10, I'll discuss the factors courts consider in deciding whether to allow such a move.

Child Support Is Always Modifiable

Courts view child support as a source that can be tapped to assure the welfare of a dependent child. Although a custodial parent may forever waive alimony or an interest in a piece of property, she can't permanently waive child support; a court can always take a fresh look and decide that the child needs financial support from the noncustodial parent.

If you're one of the 3.4 million mothers raising children alone with no court order of child support, it's not too late to get one, if you can locate your ex and establish his ability to pay. In many states this can be done by an expedited administrative procedure conducted by a hearing officer or referee of the court, rather than a judge. Your lawyer or your local child support enforcement office can guide you through the process. If you're an unwed mother, you'll need to establish paternity first.

The amount of child support, too, isn't written in stone. If a custodial parent can show that court-ordered support is inadequate, or that the noncustodial parent is making more money than at the time of the divorce or breakup, the court may order an increase in support.

Modification is a double-edged sword. If something can be changed, it can be changed in either direction—so check out the facts before you act. Suppose your ex-husband arrives to pick up the kids in a new Jaguar convertible. You figure he must be making more money, and you file for more child support. It turns out that the car was a gift from his fiancée, and he's actually earning less than before. All your petition accomplishes is to elicit a counterpetition to get his support obligation reduced.

Of course, even if you've done nothing to precipitate it, your ex may petition for a reduction or abatement of support based on changed circumstances like a job loss or salary cut. Courts are protectors of children, yes; but they also must strive to be fair to both parents.

Is Something Missing From Your Decree?

Many times, due to shortsightedness or poor draftsmanship, important questions weren't originally dealt with; loose ends that weren't thought through were left hanging. There may be no provision for medical insurance for the ex-spouse and children, or for making them beneficiaries of life insurance. There may be no provision for what happens if the parent carrying insurance coverage at work gets laid off. There may be no provision for who pays for braces; for extraordinary medical expenses; for private or parochial school, special education, college, or summer camp; for help if a child falls behind in school;

or for counseling if a child begins to show psychological problems.

Sometimes the noncustodial parent will be happy to pay for these "overlooked items" if they're called to his attention. Or he may offer to do it in return for reduced child support. But sometimes there's no way to settle the issue except through litigation.

What determines the outcome of such a lawsuit? The same factors that apply in all child support modifications: the child's needs and the parents' comparative abilities to pay. Obviously, both factors must be considered. It's all well and good to say that a child needs tutoring, but what if the father is unemployed? You can't squeeze blood from a stone. If a man is financially able to contribute, though, and the need is substantial, he doesn't have much of a defense.

The issue of college education for adult children is an interesting one. Although a child of married parents has no legal right to higher education, statutes in some (but not all) states establish such a right for a child of divorced parents. In Illinois, for example, an adult child can seek financial assistance with college expenses from either parent, depending on his or her finances. (I know of a father who never received so much as a Father's Day card from his daughter and suddenly got hit with a $13,000 tuition bill!)

Is There Anything Concerning Children That Can't Be Changed?

There are very few exceptions to the general rule that anything concerning the welfare of a child is subject to change.

One exception occurs if you give your child up for adoption, either to the other parent or to someone else. In that case, unless you can claim fraud or coercion, by voluntarily consenting to the adoption you've waived your rights to the child forever. Similarly, if you've remarried and your ex has let you and your new spouse adopt the child, your ex can't come back later and try to get custody.

You or your ex may have lost your parental rights. That might happen if one of you claimed that the other was mistreating or neglecting the child and a court found that the abuse or neglect was so extreme as to constitute, in effect, a forfeiture of parental rights. The way this typically happens is in a contested adoption suit brought by the noncustodial parent or other family member against the custodial parent. Here, as in an uncontested adoption, the only way to get back the parental rights would be a nullification action challenging the validity of the legal procedure by which they were lost.

Some decrees specify that child support is to end when a certain event occurs; for example, when the child reaches age 18 or moves out of the family home or joins the armed services or gets married. These are called **emancipation events,** and once they take place, the parent who had custody generally can't go back and claim that the child isn't really emancipated. If marriage was agreed to be an emancipation event, and if your married son brings his bride home to live with you, you can't seek restoration of child support, claiming that he's still a dependent.

Even if an emancipation event wasn't specified, when a child reaches the statutory age of majority (age 18 in most states) it's usually too late to seek a modification. So, if your 18-year-old daughter drops out of college and comes home to live, it's up to you to work out a support arrangement with her; your ex is probably out of the picture. One exception: if there's nothing in your decree about who pays for your son's or daughter's college education, and you live in one of the states with laws providing that parents must contribute to their offspring's college education according to their ability to pay, you can apply to a court to add this requirement to your decree or order even if the child is no longer a minor.

A finding of paternity is usually not modifiable. But I've had cases in which, after a divorce, an ex-husband finds out that he wasn't the child's father. He asks for blood tests, which confirm that he can't be the father. He may be able to go back and have the decree modified to eliminate his support obligation.

Alimony: Phasing It Out or Getting More

Besides matters having to do with children, the other fertile area for modification is alimony, or spousal maintenance. In 1979, the United States Supreme Court held in *Orr v. Orr* that alimony laws based on gender are unconstitutional. Thus either ex-spouse may be required to pay alimony to the other. Usually, though, it's the woman who has less earning power, especially during the childbearing and childraising years, so it's she who is more likely to be awarded maintenance. For convenience, then, I'll refer to the party paying alimony as he and the party receiving it as she.

Years ago, a lot of women got what was called **permanent alimony**. Very few of these "permanent" arrangements are holding up these days. A lot of men accepted or were saddled with open-ended alimony commitments at a time when women customarily didn't work outside the home. It was assumed that a divorced woman would remain financially dependent on her ex-husband for the indefinite future. Now that the majority of women are in the work force, judicial attitudes toward spousal maintenance have changed dramatically. Unless a woman is elderly and unskilled or is disabled, or unless she gave up property rights in exchange for the promise of alimony, she'll have a tough time collecting those payments for the rest of her life.

The trend is to expect a divorced woman to "rehabilitate herself"; that is, to become employable and at least partially self-supporting within a reasonable period of time (say, five years). If a woman makes no serious effort to do so, she's in danger of losing her maintenance. Rather than cutting her off immediately without a dime, the court may gradually reduce her maintenance or put a cap on it.

To underline the need for rehabilitation, more and more courts these days are ordering **reviewable maintenance**. For example, a court may order a man, after a 30-year marriage, to pay his ex-wife $1,000 a month, reviewable after 3 years. Such orders have become very common recently. In effect, the court is saying to the woman, "We're going to take a look three years from now and see what you've done to help yourself." As the end of the term approaches, the woman may wonder where she stands. What does reviewable mean? Is she still going to be entitled to maintenance or isn't she? On what basis? In a sense, the review is an automatic modification procedure, which could be viewed as practically a new trial.

It's also possible for a woman to get increased maintenance—or even to begin getting it for the first time—due to changed circumstances. For example, if she becomes acutely ill and can't work, a judge might order her ex-husband to contribute to her support until she's back on her feet again.

Nonmodifiable Alimony

If, at the time maintenance was awarded, it was designated as "nonmodifiable," it can't be changed later. Why would a couple have agreed to nonmodifiable maintenance? Let's consider a typical case.

Brad and Bonnie had been married for 25 years. They hadn't managed to accumulate much in the way of stocks, bonds, or other liquid assets; their major assets were the house, in which their equity was $50,000, and his pension, which amounted to $45,000. So the property division was pretty cut-and-dried; he got the pension and she got the house. Their children were grown, so child support wasn't an issue. The only remaining question was maintenance for her.

Bonnie felt she was entitled to some kind of secure financial settlement out of her long-term marriage. If there had been more assets involved, alimony might not have been so crucial; but as things were, it was all she could count on—and she wanted to be able to count on it, at least for a limited, foreseeable amount of time. Her main concern was getting through the next five years; her mother was terminally ill, and Bonnie wanted to be free to devote full time to caring for her. After her mother was gone, Bonnie figured, she'd be able to go out and get a job. Even if she remarried during the first five years after the divorce, she didn't want to forfeit her alimony. She couldn't be sure that a second marriage would last, and if she lost her rights to maintenance from the first, longtime marriage, where would she be?

Brad, at the same time, felt that he had the potential for high future earnings. He didn't want to leave open the possibility that Bonnie would come back at him for more alimony, as she might be able to do if maintenance was left modifiable. He preferred to settle for a fixed, limited obligation with a definite end in sight.

So, for both Brad and Bonnie, nonmodifiable maintenance made sense at the time of the divorce. But if some factor in the equation later changed—for example, Bonnie's mother lived longer than expected, or Brad lost his job a year after the divorce—neither of them could come back and try to change the deal. Thus couples considering nonmodifiable maintenance need to ask themselves whether they can imagine any circumstance under which they'll be sorry, and then weigh that against what they expect to gain.

Was Maintenance Waived, Reserved, or Left Open?

As I said, it may be possible to institute or modify maintenance months or even years after a decree is signed. But if you've specifically waived your right to it (presumably in exchange for something else, like a share in your ex-husband's business), you've probably lost your chance forever. If you later change your mind, it's too bad. A waiver is a waiver, and if you agreed to it voluntarily with full knowledge and without coercion, you're stuck with it.

Your lawyer may have reserved the question of maintenance for future determination. Let's say your husband happened to be out of work or earning very little at the time of the divorce. Your attorney may have advised that you shouldn't permanently waive your rights just because your husband couldn't afford to pay alimony at the moment—especially if he had been a good provider in the past. If alimony was reserved, you have a nice ace in the hole to play at an appropriate moment.

Courts often reserve maintenance (and child support and property division, too) in default divorces obtained by one party in the other's absence (usually either because the missing party can't be found or doesn't respond). The court can't put an absent person under financial obligation but may reserve judgment on money questions in case that party is later located and brought into court.

If maintenance wasn't specifically waived or reserved, and the decree is silent on the matter, the question is left open.

Recently a woman came to see me because her ex-husband's child support payments had been slacking off. She was really struggling. When I read her decree, I discovered that there was no mention of alimony. I was able to get the court not only to reinstate child support but to award her maintenance as well.

A Few More Pointers

•Everything I've said underlines the importance of reading your decree, order, or agreement carefully and having your lawyer do so periodically. Whether something is or isn't modifiable may depend on the exact language in the document.

•Don't think that because something is "nonmodifiable" it can never be changed. Even though a court won't order a modification sought by one party, the two of you can always decide to renegotiate, and if you agree, the court will issue an order incorporating the change.

That applies to property division, which courts normally don't modify. Suppose a woman loses her job and requests an increase in maintenance. Her ex may instead offer (and she may accept) an additional lump sum property settlement of $20,000 in return for a permanent waiver of maintenance after the next two years. It's something he doesn't have to do, but it may be worth it to him to do it in lieu of additional maintenance.

•You may want to seek a modification if a change in the law alters the impact of your decree, order, or agreement. For example, as I'll explain in chapter 15, you may be able to seek a modification that takes into account a change in tax rules.

•Statutes, precedents, or the language of your decree, order, or agreement, may dictate time limits on modifications. For example, your decree may provide that maintenance is reserved for three years, and after that, if it's not brought up, it's automatically waived. An issue like college education may be left open only until a child reaches a certain age. Sometimes such restrictions are written into law; sometimes they're based on considerations of equity (fairness). (Laches is an equity principle which dictates that even where there's no statute of limitations, you can't wait indefinitely to bring up a matter. After a reasonable period of time has elapsed, a court may hold that laches has set in and you're barred from proceeding.)

Third Party Modifications

You and your ex aren't the only ones who can seek to modify your decree, order, or agreement. Third parties may be able to set a modification in motion, particularly with regard to visitation and custody. For example, most states now recognize grandparents' rights to visitation with a grandchild after a divorce. Yet most decrees don't address this question, which may arise if a custodial parent decides to move out of state or refuses to let the former in-laws see the child. Grandparents may initiate a modification to provide for their visitation rights. In some cases, when both parents were unable or unwilling to properly care for the child, grandparents have sought and won custody. (More on grandparents' rights in chapter 12.)

In one unusual third-party case, my client, who claimed to be the natural father of a three-year-old girl, intervened in a custody dispute between the mother and her ex-husband. He decided to get involved when he heard that the two were charging each other with child abuse and were fighting over child support. A blood test showed that there was a 99.5 percent chance that my client was the girl's father, and he offered to contribute to the child's support. The court ultimately awarded him joint custody with the mother and her ex—as far as I know, the first case of triple joint custody.

Court-Initiated Modifications

The court itself can order a modification that wasn't requested by the parties. Suppose a father was originally awarded nightly visitation. He comes into court complaining that his ex isn't letting him see the child that often. The court may say, yes, technically she's in contempt—but such frequent visitation really isn't in the child's best interests. Even though the decree provided for it, the judge may take a hard look at the situation, conclude that nightly visitation just isn't going to work, and decide to change it.

Of course, the mother could have asked for the change on her own, or in response to her ex-husband's complaint. But perhaps she wasn't properly represented, or her attorney chose not to rock the boat. The court is responsible for overseeing the child's welfare and can't have its hands tied by a party's failure to raise an issue.

By the same token, when there has been flagrant, chronic violation of visitation rights with a string of transparent excuses, a court may order a change of custody even though the other parent didn't request it. I've seen a court amend a support award, too. Suppose a noncustodial parent is obligated to pay far beyond his means. Either he didn't have a lawyer in the first place or his lawyer didn't think to seek a modification. When the custodial parent tries to enforce the award, the court may instead reduce it. In effect, the judge may say, "I don't know how this happened to begin with, but I'm going to fix it."

A court can't do anything (or even know anything) about a problem unless and until someone brings something to the court's attention. But once an issue is brought up, the court has broad power to impose modifications. So think twice before opening Pandora's box: if you're thinking of filing a petition to enforce or modify your decree, discuss with your lawyer any feature of your situation that might cause such action to boomerang.

On the other hand, if you really feel that you're being treated unfairly, don't hesitate to seek a legal remedy. Every case is worth pursuing if you believe you have a good point. Even if the law seems to be against you, a good lawyer may be able to persuade a court to see things your way. A court of equity will listen to almost any reasonable argument. What the law is today is not necessarily what the law will be tomorrow; and many changes in the law result from some ingenious lawyer's filing some creative pleading that catches a court's attention. That's part of the excitement of the work I do—seeing some new twist every day.

Now that I've outlined the basic principles governing modification, let's look at the most common categories of modifications—custody, child support, alimony, and visitation—in more detail.

8

GAINING AND KEEPING CUSTODY

"I'm going to take the children away from you!" This threat, spoken or unspoken, haunts many custodial parents.

Custody can be one of the most heart-wrenching issues connected with a divorce or the breakup of a relationship between unwed parents, and it's an issue that isn't irrevocably resolved until a child comes of age. The victor in a custody battle can never rest easy, for the tables can be turned if at any time someone—the noncustodial parent, a grandparent, another relative, child welfare authorities, the police, or someone else—can show a court sufficient reason.

The factors that affect a change in custody are complex and depend very much on the circumstances of a particular case. In this chapter, I'll give you an idea of the kinds of questions courts look at and the principles they follow in custody disputes that arise after a divorce decree or custody order has been entered. Although custody is sometimes awarded to someone other than the parent, I'll be talking mainly about situations in which ex-spouses or ex-lovers are fighting over custody of a child.

Custody: Not for Women Only

In the United States, women traditionally have been awarded custody, especially of young children, under the presumption that a child of "tender years" is usually best off with the mother unless she's clearly unfit. In recent years, legislatures and courts have moved to eliminate gender bias by substituting for the "tender years" doctrine a standard based on "the best interests of the child." The proportion of custody awards to fathers has risen, and an increasing number of states now allow joint custody.

A growing number of women are recognizing that in some situations everyone concerned may be better off if the children live with their father. This may be true, for example, if the father was the one who was more involved with the children before the divorce, if the children seem to be happier with the father, if the mother feels a need for a release from the primary burdens of childraising or admits that she wasn't cut out for mothering, or if the father's working hours are more flexible than the mother's.

Still, according to 1986 census figures, 89 percent of the 14.8 million children in single-parent households live with the mother and only 11 percent with the father. Because it's the mother who usually has custody in the first place, in the majority of contested change-of-custody cases it's the father who's seeking the change and the mother who's trying to hold onto the child. So, unless it's clearly the other way around, I'll refer to the custodial parent (the one having custody) as she and the noncustodial parent (the one seeking custody) as he. Keep in mind, though, that the parties to a custody dispute aren't necessarily limited to the parents. Grandparents or others may be involved.

How Courts Decide on Custody

Just what does "the best interests of the child" mean, and how do courts determine which custodian would be in the child's best interests? Definitions vary somewhat from state to state but are typically taken or adapted from the Uniform Dissolution of Marriage Act.

In Michigan, for example, the law takes into consideration the emotional ties between each of the disputing parties and the child; their ability and willingness to give the child love, affection, guidance, education, and religious training, as well as food, clothing, medical care, and other material necessities; the length of time a child has lived in a stable, satisfactory environment, and the desirability of maintaining continuity; the permanence of the family units in the existing and proposed custodial homes; the moral fitness and mental and physical health of the contesting parties; the child's record at home, at school, and in the community; the willingness and ability of each parent to encourage a close and continuing relationship between the child and the other parent; and any other relevant factors.

In neighboring Wisconsin, the standards are slightly different. There, courts must consider the wishes of the parents; the child's relationship with parents, siblings, and others; the child's social adjustment; the mental and physical health of the parties and of any children or other members of their households; availability of child care; and any other relevant factors.

In both Michigan and Wisconsin, along with most other states, the court may consider the child's wishes, assuming the child is old enough to express a preference. How much weight a court gives to the child's preference depends on the child's age and maturity.

Considerations and Procedures in a Custody Change

The same factors that determine custody in the first place will normally apply when a court considers a change of custody. However, because stability is important for a child, most states make it more difficult to seek a change of custody within a certain period after a custody determination. In Illinois, for example, unless you can prove that the child is physically or emotionally endangered, you can't seek a change in a custody order for two years from the date of that order. The purpose of such restrictions is to avoid subjecting a child to an ongoing custody feud, with one party or the other coming in for a change of custody every few months.

Endangerment is comparatively easy to assess. But once the standard becomes the best interests of the child, a court's judgment in many cases is highly subjective. The court must balance factors that may add up to six of one and half a dozen of the other.

The questions a court may consider include: Which parent is better able to provide for the child? Which is more able to personally care for the child? How healthy an environment can each create? What schooling and religious training options can and will each make available? If a special school seems advisable, does one parent live conveniently near such a school? How nearby are the child's friends and extended family? These are not really legal issues, and the answers are seldom black and white. There are many gray areas, and a custody decision is often a close call.

To help weigh these and other factors, courts tend to rely heavily on input from psychologists and social workers who have interviewed the child and the parents and may have visited the existing and proposed custodial homes. Four states— California, Delaware, Maine, and Wisconsin—require mediation before a change of custody (or other divorce-related judgment) can be entered, and 18 states permit a court to order mediation.

In some states a judge can (and in New Hampshire and Wisconsin the judge must) appoint a guardian ad litem to represent the child's interests and present the matter from the child's perspective: in effect, to "stand in" for a minor in court. In some instances, the guardian ad litem may interview the child in more relaxed surroundings than the formal atmosphere of a courtroom and then make recommendations to the court. The guardian ad litem won't necessarily argue for what the child wants (or says he or she wants) but must strive to represent the child's best interests. Although the guardian ad litem need not be an attorney, generally a single person is appointed who can act both as guardian ad litem and as attorney for the child and thus can make motions, obtain depositions, and take other legal steps on the child's behalf. So technically the guardian ad litem and the attorney for the child are separate roles and can be separate people, but for simplicity's sake I'll refer to the person who generally performs both functions as guardian ad litem.

The purpose of all these measures is not only to help achieve the best possible resolution of the issues but to insulate the child against a full-blown custody battle, in which the child's interests may get lost in a clash of parental wills.

Still, custody disputes often result in bitter recriminations not only against the other party but against the court system itself. "Unfair!" cries a father who couldn't get custody because the judge insisted that a two-year-old girl needs her mother. "Unfair!" cries a mother whose son was taken away twice—once by her ex-husband, who abducted him, and then by the court, which found that her clinical depression, brought on by the child-snatching, made her unfit to care for the boy.

Certainly there are miscarriages of justice. Judges aren't all-knowing or all-wise, and neither are psychologists and social workers. But it's also more than slightly possible for a parent's perception of the situation to be colored by emotion.

To help you assess more accurately your chances of gaining or keeping custody, let's look at some of the most common reasons why custody changes occur. When there's a change of custody, it's usually safe to assume that one of three things has happened. Either there has been a drastic change in the custodial parent's life, in the noncustodial parent's life, or in the child's wishes or circumstances.

When the Custodial Parent's Life Changes

Probably the majority of change-of-custody cases turn on the question of whether the custodial parent is still the proper person to have custody. The issue usually arises from something in that person's behavior—something she's doing or not doing or the people she's associating with, such as a new husband or boyfriend.

A court is likely to presume that the custodial parent's behavior will directly or indirectly affect the child. Sometimes that presumption is borne out by specific evidence, such as obvious signs of abuse or neglect, which will almost inevitably result in loss of custody. More often, the evidence is indirect. A sudden drop in the child's school grades may suggest that something is seriously wrong in the child's life, and a court may infer that the child is upset about the mother's remarriage. Sometimes, even though the custodial parent's actions (for example, taking a lover who's on drugs) have so far had no discernible effect on the child, the court views the new situation as holding the potential for harm.

The Double Standard of Parenting

"Neglect" in a custody case doesn't necessarily mean that a child is abandoned, going hungry, or coming to school in tatters. A custodial parent may be found to be neglecting a child if, for example, the child regularly comes home to an empty house after school or is constantly left with babysitters, friends, or relatives.

Unfair? Perhaps. Many parents these days use day care or make latchkey arrangements for their school-age children. If the parent isn't divorced or separated and the child isn't under court jurisdiction, no one is likely to interfere. But once a child comes under judicial protection, as in a divorce case, the court has a high level of interest in the child's well-being and an involvement in many aspects of the child's life. So, if a court awards custody to a mother with the understanding that she's going to be taking care of her child and then finds that the child is continually left alone or with someone else, the court's view of who is the more fit parent may change.

Custody Changes Often Reflect Changes in Relationships

Many times a modification is simply a reflection of what's actually happening. Suppose a custodial mother begins taking a course, or her work requires her to go to out-of-town conferences, or maybe she just has an active social schedule. Her ex and the children have a good relationship, his working hours are flexible, and more and more she finds herself dropping off the children with him. Eventually he may ask himself, "Why am I paying child support? I might as well have custody and let her pay me." In such a case, the court is merely called upon to recognize and ratify a change in the parties' relationships that has already occurred.

Lifestyles and Labels

If a custodial parent takes a live-in lover, marries someone of a different race or religion, enters into a homosexual relationship, or has been convicted of a criminal offense, what are the chances of losing custody? At one time, they would have been virtually 100 percent. But times, societal attitudes, and court precedents have changed.

Ten or fifteen years ago, cohabitation, in and of itself, was grounds for denial of custody. Today that's no longer true, because unwed relationships are no longer so shocking.

The nation's highest court in 1984 stepped into another sensitive issue. In *Palmore v. Sidoti*, the Supreme Court held that it was unconstitutional for a Florida court to take custody away from a white mother because of her remarriage to a black man. The Florida court had said that the child would inevitably suffer from the prevailing social stigma against interracial marriage. But the Supreme Court ruled that race cannot be a factor in modifying custody and that the effect of community racial prejudice can't be considered.

Today courts almost unanimously avoid using stereotypes as the basis for custody determinations and instead consider the evidence on a case-by-case basis. If, for example, a custodial parent takes a gay lover, that fact alone won't be enough to dictate a change of custody. The person seeking custody will have to show, probably through expert testimony, how that circumstance may adversely affect the child.

That's not to say that justice is evenhanded when it comes to unpopular lifestyles. As I said, what's in the best interests of a child is a subjective decision on a judge's part. And judges, like all human beings, have biases, which are influenced by prevailing community standards. In fact, in most parts of the country, if there's a gay lover in the picture, there's probably a 95 percent chance that the custodial parent will end up losing the child— even though studies, such as one done at the University of California at Los Angeles, have found no greater tendency toward homosexuality or developmental problems in children raised by gay mothers.

Similarly, a custodial parent who takes a child to live in a commune or joins a cult or a white supremacy group like the Ku Klux Klan may be jeopardizing custody. Isn't this a free country? Yes, but under certain circumstances a child's health or welfare may become the subject of judicial concern. For example, parents who are Jehovah's Witnesses or practitioners of Christian Science have been forced to accept medical care for their child despite their religious beliefs.

In a custody case, the child comes under the jurisdiction of the court, and the court can scrutinize any aspect of the custodial parent's behavior to see whether it's in the child's best interests. If the custodial parent does something that shocks the sensibilities of the judge, and if someone (like the noncustodial parent) brings that behavior to the court's attention, a change of custody may ensue.

When the Noncustodial Parent's Life Changes

Martha had custody of her two children, ten-year-old Peter and six-year-old Matthew. Although their three-room apartment was rather cramped, it was the best Martha could do with the minimal child support she got from her ex-husband, David. The court-ordered support was all David could afford at the time, and even though he was making more money now, she didn't want the hassle of going back to court to ask for more. With her teacher's salary, she was able to make ends meet, and the job allowed her to be home when her boys were. Peter and Matthew seemed happy and well-adjusted and were doing fine in school. Their relationship with both their mother and their father, who lived a few miles away, was very good.

Then David, who had recently remarried, got a promotion. He and his new wife moved into a six-room house and decided that they would like to have the boys live with them. So he filed for a change of custody.

What would a court decide? Could a father's improved financial circumstances and his ability to provide a larger, more comfortable home outweigh the evidence that the present situation was working well? Certainly it could. But it's also possible that the mother might countersue for more child support, and the court might grant it and leave the children undisturbed. For that reason, in most cases a man would be ill advised to bring such a suit.

This hypothetical example brings up a sensitive issue: the role that the parties' financial status plays in custody decisions. In some cases (for example, in Maryland and the District of Columbia) fathers who failed to pay child support have been able to turn around and use their superior economic position as a lever for a custody change. On the other hand, the Wisconsin Supreme Court in a 1984 case (*Gould v. Gould*) held it improper for a court to consider which parent can more easily provide material advantages. In reversing a lower court's award of custody to the father, the court stated: "While the economic well-being of children of divorced parents must be provided for, it is best achieved by the Court's making appropriate child support and maintenance awards and by focusing judicial resources on enforcement of awards and not by considering financial ability as a criterion for custody."

When Does a Change of Heart Lead To a Change of Custody?

Most of the time, as I said, the mother gets custody at the outset—assuming she wants it. But what if she doesn't, and then changes her mind?

I've had several cases in which a mother who initiated a breakup wanted out so badly that she gave the father the house and the children and just walked away. She didn't feel that she could deal with a two-year contested divorce proceeding. He was the breadwinner, and since she didn't have a job, a place to live, or the wherewithal to take care of the children, it made more sense for them to stay with him. Then she went back to school, got a job, found an apartment, became self-sufficient, or remarried. Now she felt capable of caring for her children, and she wanted them back.

Such a situation was dramatized in the movie *Kramer v. Kramer*. The mother, played by Meryl Streep, felt unable to cope with marriage and motherhood and needed time to find herself. The father, played by Dustin Hoffman, had some rocky moments as a single parent but eventually established a warm, wholesome relationship with his little boy. Then Streep came back into the picture, insisting she wanted the child back. She won in court but backed away tearfully when she finally realized that she'd be breaking up the home in which her son was happy.

The outcome of that screen trial may have been good drama, but it was unconvincing. The mother simply didn't have enough evidence. The difficulties Hoffman was having in balancing his roles of custodial father and breadwinner were no more than any single parent might expect, and Streep never showed why the boy would be better off with her.

Kramer v. Kramer may have had an impact in advancing the cause of fathers' rights. My feeling is that if a case like that were tried today, the mother wouldn't get the child. Other things being equal, a mother may initially have an edge in a custody determination; but once custody has been established, the status quo has the edge. A court normally won't upset a stable situation unless there's good reason to do so. It's not enough for a mother to arrive out of the blue and announce, "Here I am! I'm ready to raise my child."

There are some situations in which a court might decide to grant a mother's belated wish for custody. What if the father is struggling not very successfully to take care of the child? What if the mother is clearly the better parent but simply needed some time at first to get on her feet? What if the child wants to be with the mother? These and other factors might influence a court in her favor.

I had a paternity case in which a 19-year-old unwed mother let the father have custody of the infant. The father was a 40-year-old doctor, well-to-do and willing to make a home for the baby. The mother was young, frightened, insecure, and unready for the responsibilities of motherhood. A few years later, when she had finished college and married, she was able to provide a proper home for the child and convinced a court to give her a chance.

When the Child's Wishes and Circumstances Change

Eleven-year-old Daniel has been living with his mother since he was two. He's doing all right, but he wants to get to know his father better than he can on twice-weekly visits. At Daniel's request, his father files for a change of custody. What will the court decide?

We can't be sure, because every case is different; but in general, the older and more mature a child is, the more a court will take the child's desires into account. Some eleven-year-olds are almost adult-like, while others act like eight-year-olds. On the other hand, some eight-year-olds are mature enough to convince a judge that they know their own minds.

If Daniel seems immature, his wishes won't carry much weight against the court's view of his best interests. Children's testimony can be unreliable. If Daniel says he's tired of living with Mommy, is it because he's temporarily angry at Mommy—perhaps for punishing him severely? Or could it be that Daddy has brainwashed Daniel into saying he wants to live with him, either through threats or promises?

I once had a case in which my client's ex-husband, a big, burly police sergeant, wanted custody of his four sons. The boys, who were eight to twelve years old, said they wanted to live with their father. At my suggestion, the court agreed to interview all four youngsters in chambers. One after another, they came in, and it was like a recording—they all said exactly the same thing. It was obvious to the judge, to me, and even to the father's attorney that this man had intimidated his sons; they were all scared to death. Finally they broke down under the judge's questioning and admitted that they had been coached by their father.

Here's where the guardian ad litem can be very helpful. In this case, the judge gave the children the phone number of the guardian ad litem, so that if their father tried to take his disappointment out on them, they would have someone to turn to for protection.

By the time a young person reaches adolescence, his or her wishes are usually the overriding concern in a custody suit. A teenaged boy who isn't getting along with his mother may take matters into his own hands. He may simply show up on his father's doorstep, duffel in tow, and say, "Hi, Dad, I want to live with you." A court is likely to go along—unless the mother can show that the youngster is emotionally disturbed or is trying to avoid discipline. (I've seen kids who bounced back and forth from parent to parent, trying to get the best deal. Courts don't look favorably on such manipulation.)

A youngster's case is strengthened when his or her wishes tie in with special needs and circumstances. For example, Lisa has recently shown a flair for art. There's a topflight school within a mile of her mother's house, whereas if she stays with her father, she'll have to take three buses clear across the city to get to class. Rick has joined the high-school tennis team and wants to live with his father, a former pro, so Dad can more closely guide his training. Unless there are important factors pointing in another direction, a judge is likely to grant a change of custody in such cases.

Remarriage or Cohabitation May Trigger a Custody Change

The remarriage of either parent or the marriage of an unwed parent can lead to a change of custody. The same is true when the custodial parent begins cohabiting, especially if the lover has a family of his own.

Sometimes children don't get along with their mother's new husband or lover and his children. They decide that they want to live with their "real" father. Perhaps a 16-year-old stepbrother starts molesting a 10-year-old girl, and her father finds out about it and files for custody. Maybe a stepfather is a stern disciplinarian and spanks his wife's child, and that doesn't sit well with the father. A mother may be so busy trying to adjust to her new family responsibilities that she's less attentive to her own children, or her love life may suddenly become more important to her than anything else. These and many other circumstances can trigger a loss of custody. On the other side of the coin, a noncustodial parent's remarriage may make it possible to offer a more stable home for the child.

How Often Are Custody Suits Successful?

It's almost impossible to tell. Many cases are settled out of court. But my impression is that the percentage of victories is fairly high, because many cases are screened right in the lawyer's office. A good lawyer won't take a custody case unless the grounds appear to be pretty solid. Filing a frivolous action can result in penalties for both lawyer and client. An effective screening step in some states is mandatory mediation, which can weed out the serious custody cases from those involving short-term problems that may be alleviated without a change of custody.

The trend is away from viewing custody as a win-lose situation. Many times when a father is asking for a change of custody, his underlying aim is to achieve better parenting for the child. He may be reluctant to file for a custody change but sees no alternative. He doesn't really want custody, but the situation as he perceives it has deteriorated to the point where he feels he must do something about it.

In some cases, a father may not be successful in getting a complete change of custody; he may be satisfied if he gets joint custody or more visitation. Even if there's no legal modification, the process itself may have a beneficial effect. For example, let's say the mother is using part of her child support money to support an irresponsible lover and the father blows the whistle through a custody suit. Now she's faced with a choice: either get this man out of her life or lose custody. If she does throw the bum out and keep the child, was the father's suit successful? Yes, in the sense that he produced a positive change in the child's life.

Avoiding Custody Battles

Some custody fights can't be avoided. If you have reason to believe that your child is being physically, sexually, or psychologically abused or is being exposed to clearly harmful influences such as pornography or drugs, and if your ex refuses to change her behavior but wants to hold onto the child, you have no choice but to act as quickly as possible. But most of the cases I've described in this chapter are far less clear-cut.

Often the real motivation behind a custody suit is that the noncustodial parent feels shut out of the child's life. One way to prevent resentment that can snowball into a custody issue is to keep the noncustodial parent informed—for example, about how the child is doing in school. If a child has earned a swimming letter or made the honor roll or is in the school play, the noncustodial parent has a right to know. (Even without the cooperation of the custodial parent, a noncustodial parent should be able to get information directly from the school. Parents don't need to be custodians to receive copies of the child's report cards or progress reports, or to request a conference with the teacher.)

To Sum Up

If you're determined to seek a custody change, or if you're forced to defend against one, the points I've discussed in this chapter should help you assess and perhaps improve your chances of winning.

Joint custody is a solution often touted these days to avoid custody battles. In the next chapter we'll examine how well it works.

9

WHEN JOINT CUSTODY DOESN'T WORK

Perhaps the earliest recorded example of a custody dispute is the Biblical story of two women who came before King Solomon, both claiming the same baby. Solomon threw up his hands and ordered the child cut in two, whereupon one woman begged him to let the other have the infant. "Ah," said Solomon, "now I can see who is the true mother," and awarded the child to the woman who had been willing to give it up rather than see it harmed.

Modern-day Solomons have found another alternative to the trauma of a custody battle: joint custody. Usually (but not always) the parties sharing custody are the child's parents. (I've previously mentioned an unusual case in which custody was shared three ways, between the mother, her estranged husband, and her lover, the natural father.)

The idea behind joint custody sounds sensible. A man and woman who break up with each other aren't breaking up with their child. Why shouldn't the child continue to have the benefit of both parents' care? Just because they don't want to be married or to live together anymore, why can't two civilized people cooperate in rearing their child?

Unfortunately, it often doesn't work out that way. In this chapter, I'll discuss the pluses and minuses of joint custody, what determines its success or failure, and what to do if it's not working.

What Is Joint Custody?

First let's get our terms straight. Joint (or shared) custody doesn't necessarily mean that a child lives with both parents or splits the time equally between them. **Joint residential custody** (or joint physical possession) is very unusual and not very workable unless the parents live near each other and get along extremely well.

In close to 95 percent of cases, joint custody means **joint legal custody.** Both parents are supposed to decide questions concerning the child's health, education, and welfare and to participate in the child's upbringing. Usually, however, the child's daily life isn't materially different than under sole custody. The child lives with one parent and visits with the other; though visitation rights may be more extensive under joint custody and may be called something else, such as "time with the child."

The Trend Toward Joint Custody

Joint custody is a product of the gender revolution. Before the 1970s, the almost universal pattern was for the mother to get sole custody. The women's movement promoted a breakdown of rigidly gender-based activities and attitudes. Not only could women be lawyers and bricklayers—men could be caregivers. It was a logical progression from interchangeable roles to men's rights. Fathers began to say, "I'm a parent too. Why shouldn't I have custody, or at least an equal voice in important decisions that affect my child?" And some mothers began to recognize that they needed and wanted to share the responsibilities of childraising.

At first, joint custody awards were almost always the result of voluntary agreement between the parties. Joint custody was a new and untried concept, and parents who wanted it usually had to "sell" a reluctant judge. But within the past decade, joint custody has caught on fast; most states have adopted it through case law or legislation or both. Joint custody is not only permitted but encouraged and may even be imposed on unwilling parents. In many states, joint custody is now presumed to be in the best interests of the child, and a parent who doesn't want to share custody has the burden of showing why not.

The chief rationale for joint custody is that, to minimize the shock of a breakup, children should not be deprived of either parent. Instead, they should have as much access and preserve as normal a relationship as possible with both. Joint custody also can prevent either parent from feeling shut out or being labeled unfit. Fathers' rights advocates say that joint custody enables fathers to remain more actively involved in their children's lives. Some studies suggest that boys who suffer from diminished contact with their fathers may do better in joint custody arrangements.

As legislatures and courts have climbed on the bandwagon, some observers have questioned whether most estranged or divorced couples can or will cooperate well enough to make joint custody work. Women's organizations say that some mothers have been forced to accept joint parenting against their wishes and that children caught between conflicting parents have been harmed. Contrary to the claim advanced by fathers' groups that men who have joint custody are more likely to live up to their support obligations, the women's groups argue that joint custody is sometimes used to justify inadequate child support awards or as a bargaining lever to deter women from seeking better money settlements.

Now the trend may be shifting the other way. The California legislature, which adopted a pioneering joint custody statute in 1979, declared in August 1988 that courts should make "neither a preference nor a presumption" for joint custody. Instead, judges are to consider all custody options. The California legislature's action was influenced by recent studies challenging the success of some joint custody arrangements. This research also may prompt other states to take a second look at joint custody laws.

How Successful Is Joint Custody?

Early studies on the success of joint custody painted a glowing picture: deeply involved fathers, satisfied mothers, thriving children, and lower-than-usual rates of relitigation. But these studies were few in number, and virtually all of them covered voluntary arrangements. Now it appears that these pioneering families were highly unusual.

More recent research indicates that unless conditions are favorable (see Box 5), children under joint custody tend to be under stress; family conflict is high, and so is the likelihood of a return bout in court. Mothers complain that rather than having their burdens eased, they retain total responsibility for child care yet have to cope with interference from the father and, often, low child support awards that push them below the poverty line. Yet welfare requirements that contemplate an "absent parent" make it difficult for them to get assistance.

In one study, none of the court-imposed and court-influenced joint custody arrangements were seen as successful; the more the court had influenced the decision, the worse the outcome. Another recent study found a majority of preschoolers to be doing poorly under joint custody. One psychiatrist has reported that when joint custody is a compromise to avert parental warfare, it's virtually certain that children will develop psychological problems. Studies done in the San Francisco Bay area found that when there has been a bitter custody battle, access to both parents often increases the children's emotional distress. These researchers found that in about one-third of divorce cases, bitterness and hostility continue for several years, especially when the separation was traumatic.

These studies support my view that the trend toward imposing joint custody has been misguided. If the parties are hostile, unwilling, or uncooperative, joint custody can give them an arena and a reason to continue fighting. Childraising is a complex, demanding business. It's hard enough when parents have a good relationship; when they are constantly at each other's throats, no one benefits, least of all the child. An appropriate custody arrangement should reduce, not create tension.

The bottom line is, we're dealing with children's lives. If we truly consider what's best for a child, a presumption in favor of joint custody may be unwise. All that may be accomplished is to postpone a custody battle at the cost of perpetuating conflict in a child's life.

Don't forget, in most cases in which joint custody is court-imposed, we're talking about people who couldn't get along with each other to begin with and who may have been embroiled in animosity and vindictiveness during a divorce. How are they going to suddenly begin cooperating as joint parents?

Even when parents agree to joint custody, it's often little more than a sop to the ego or a face-saving device. Neither party walks away from the negotiating table empty-handed; neither feels that he or she has lost or given up custody. Many fathers who seek joint custody do so out of spite or to lessen their child support obligations, not because they want to be active parents. And some mothers can't accept the social stigma of giving up custody, even though they have no interest in raising a child.

Custody Isn't the Real Issue

The California studies I've mentioned, as well as others at Arizona State University and the University of Rochester, concluded that custody itself isn't as important an influence on children's emotional adjustment as are other factors such as the child's age and stage of development, the intensity of the disruption caused by the divorce, and the child's relationship with both parents and with other adults, as well as the amount of continuing conflict between the parents.

A custody decree or agreement is just a starting point. What you do with custody once you have it is what really matters.

The truth is that much of the demand for joint custody is mere lip service. How parents relate to each other and to their child has very little to do with whether they do or don't have joint legal custody. Some children under joint custody grow up in an atmosphere of constant bickering that may be destructive to their emotional health, while some children under sole custody have a good relationship with both parents and are emotionally well-adjusted.

Regardless of the type of custody, a parent who genuinely wants to participate in a child's life can usually get as much visitation as he or she wants. If a noncustodial parent sees a child frequently and participates meaningfully in the child's life, it doesn't really matter what the words say on the paper.

As for joint decision-making, most routine decisions are best handled by the parent who's on the scene—usually the mother. How often does a question come up that's important enough to require a joint decision? Apart from what school, church, or orthodontist a child is to go to, it's hard to think of many. And let's face it: if David's mother wants to send him to Hebrew school and his father wants to send him to Catholic school, they have a real problem that joint custody isn't going to solve. One recent Denver case shows the lengths to which some judges have gone in this area. The court gave a Catholic mother physical custody of her two daughters but gave "spiritual custody" to the girls' Jewish father.

Parents who have joint custody and are at odds on vital (or not-so-vital) issues are likely to wind up in stalemate or in court. Judges in such cases become super-parents, deciding (as has occurred in actual cases) where a child is to go to school or whether a child with low grades shall be allowed to ride his bicycle. At least with sole custody somebody can make decisions on a day-to-day basis.

Joint Custody Can Be Dangerous

In certain states, joint custody legislation has a "friendly parent" provision, which directs the judge, in awarding custody, to consider which parent is most likely to allow the other to have frequent contact with the child. This provision, which sounds laudable on the surface, can have the unfortunate result of continuing a child's exposure to an abusive parent, or making a woman maintain contact with a wife-beater.

How can this happen? An abuser may use the "friendly

Box 5

Joint Custody Can Work Well When . . .

- The parents want it and are committed to its success.
- The child wants it.
- Both parents have high self-esteem and are relatively secure financially.
- The child has a healthy, positive relationship with both parents.
- The parents get along well or can keep their own conflicts out of their relationships with the child.
- Disruptions in the child's daily life are kept to a minimum.
- The parents agree on the rules for the arrangement.
- The powers, rights, and duties of both parents are clearly spelled out, yet leave room for flexibility and are tailored to the individual child's needs.

Joint Custody May Not Work When . . .

- One or both parents oppose it, or the child doesn't want it.
- There is friction, conflict, anger, or hostility between the parents.
- One parent believes that the other is a bad parent.
- The parents have widely disparate lifestyles or standards of living.
- One parent is using joint custody as a wedge to harass or threaten the other parent or the child.
- The parties are unclear or rigid about their respective powers, rights, and duties.

parent" requirement as a weapon to force his ex to agree to share custody. If she resists or appears unwilling to allow liberal visitation, she may be regarded as "unfriendly" and may risk losing custody altogether, leaving her child in the clutches of the abuser. A good lawyer should be able to fight such a tactic, but sometimes a woman gives in for fear of losing custody and out of a desire to gain her freedom as quickly as possible, without getting into a long drawn-out divorce battle. Also, many women are afraid to testify about being abused and fear (sometimes with good reason) that they won't be taken seriously.

If you agreed to joint custody for such reasons and your ex is continuing to abuse you and/or your child, you should get legal help immediately. Your lawyer should be able to explain to the court the circumstances under which you accepted joint custody and to show that it's not in the child's best interests.

Making Joint Custody Work

There's no such thing as a generic joint custody order or agreement; each one is different. To maximize the chances of success and avoid some of the pitfalls of joint custody, a divorce decree or custody order should specify detailed guidelines for the parties to live by. It should state clearly with whom the child is to live and when the child will see the other parent. If the parents have joint residential custody, the decree or order should spell out when and for how long the child is to stay with each.

There may be limitations on the parents' lifestyles: for example, no overnight visits from lovers while the child is in the house. There should be provisions for communication between the parents: for example, if one is going to be out of town, a requirement to notify the other of where he or she can be reached. The decree or order should also outline the circumstances under which one parent may or may not remove the child from the state. Other items to be covered include mutual participation in school activities and decisions about medical or psychological treatment and religious training. If your decree or order doesn't cover these or other important items, or is vague, you should seek to have it modified.

The Joint Parenting Agreement or Order

In Illinois and some other states, every joint custody order must be accompanied by a separate, more detailed document called a **joint parenting agreement**, which controls each parent's powers, rights, and duties with regard to the child. Ideally, the parents should cooperate in drawing up a joint parenting agreement, but if they can't agree, the court can impose its own rules in the form of a **joint parenting order**.

The joint parenting agreement or order provides for the child's residence, the division of the child's time between the parents, how decisions are to be made, and how disputes are to be handled. It sets up procedures for any changes in the document and for dealing with any alleged violations of it. In Illinois, for example, if either party fails to live up to the agreement or order, he or she can be held in contempt of court.

A joint parenting agreement or order should provide both structure and flexibility and should take the individual child's needs into consideration. The rules should be tailor-made to the particular situation; what works for one family may not work for another. Rather than simply saying, "You take the kid on Monday, Wednesday, and Friday, I'll take her on Tuesday, Thursday, and Saturday, and we'll alternate Sundays," parents need to consider what arrangement will best suit them and their child.

I must reiterate that I have real reservations about joint custody unless the parties agree to it and can work out the details amicably. The more rules and regulations that are imposed by a court, the more chance there is for conflict. Joint custody can set up a power struggle—a never-ending battle in the courts, which creates more tension in the family and less stability for the child.

Changing Residential Custody

Joint custody, like any custody order, is always modifiable. That means that if it's not working out, you can seek sole custody, or you can give up custody, or you can retain joint custody but ask that the child live with you instead of your ex or vice versa. The latter is called a change in residential custody, or physical possession of the child.

One of the advantages of joint custody is ease of switching physical possession. Suppose a youngster who has been living with the mother wants to go to high school in the father's city. With joint custody, it's a fairly simple matter for the parents to agree on such a change. They don't even have to take any formal legal action. However, since the switch does involve a variance in the terms of the joint parenting agreement—and especially if it necessitates a change in support payments—it's wise (and not very costly) to see a lawyer and execute a simple agreed order for the court to sign. (I've said it before: verbal agreements can come back to haunt you if your ex later denies there was such an agreement.)

When the parents don't agree on a modification, a court may be called upon to make a judgment based on a change of circumstances. For example, when Johnny was seven years old, joint residential custody may have worked well. It may have been fine for him to have a room at Mom's house and one at Dad's and to ride his bike back and forth. But what happens when he's 14, it's midnight, he has a history assignment due the next day, and he realizes that the books he needs are at his mother's place and she's probably asleep? At some point, most children need and prefer to have one place they can call home.

Terminating Joint Custody

The other kind of modification occurs when the court terminates joint custody and awards sole custody to one party. You have a good basis for termination if your ex isn't living up to the terms of a joint parenting agreement or order. So, if you're unhappy with joint custody and you don't have a joint parenting agreement or order, a smart strategy is to go to court and ask for one; then try to show that your ex hasn't abided by it.

If the presumption or preference in your state is for joint custody, you'll need to amass convincing evidence of your ex's failings as a parent or the ways in which joint custody is harming your child. Keeping a journal will help you point to specific examples. You may need to call upon a psychologist as an expert witness.

Use It Or Lose It

Many times, as a tactical matter during a difficult divorce, I'll advise my client to get it over with—even if that means sharing custody—knowing that we can come back to court on the custody issue later.

During divorce negotiations, custody tends to become entangled with other issues. In one case I had, the father, Tom, threatened his wife, Linda, "If you won't give me joint custody, you'll have to sell the house, and you won't see a penny of my pension." The mother, Linda, didn't believe that Tom was genuinely interested in being a co-parent; she felt he was just using the custody dispute as a weapon. But she wasn't emotionally prepared to battle on all these fronts at the same time, or to drag out the fight for two years. I told her, "Let's give him the benefit of the doubt on custody. If he doesn't live up to his responsibilities, we'll go back and go to war on that one issue." Chances were that the court was going to order joint custody anyway. By agreeing to it, Linda gave him enough rope to hang himself.

That's just what happened. After securing joint custody and liberal visitation, Tom rarely showed up to see his daughter. After four months, his ex-wife, Linda, consulted me. "It's as though he's trying to rile me," she said. "I get Jennifer all ready, we wait and wait, and he doesn't come. He shows no interest in how she's doing at school or anything else. But then if he occasionally takes it into his head to see her, he expects me to accommodate him no matter what else is going on. Not only that—he's two months behind in his child support."

Men like Tom look upon visitation as a right, not an obligation. Normally, if a woman has sole custody, there's not much she can do if her ex chooses not to exercise his visitation rights, or to exercise them erratically, unless she can show that he's harassing her. But since Tom had joint custody, I successfully argued that he had in effect forfeited it by failing to participate meaningfully in his daughter's life.

Often, even when a man like Tom does exercise visitation, it's clear that he isn't truly interested in being involved with the children. His real interest is in his ex. A man like this may come over or telephone daily, ostensibly to discuss something about the children, when he's actually trying to harass or check up on their mother. His ego is wounded because she threw him out, so he seizes on joint custody and visitation as a way to stay in her life.

Some of these men act as if they think that joint custody gives them joint custody of the house. They come over to see the children, sit in the easy chair, and make themselves at home, acting as if they were still married. A woman can pull the rug out from under a man like this by insisting that he and the children do their visiting somewhere else. Often he'll simply stop showing up, and at that point, as in Tom's case, he may leave himself open to losing joint custody.

When Men Go for Sole Custody

Since the woman usually has the children living with her, she's more frequently the one who moves for a change from joint to sole custody. Occasionally, though, the shoe is on the other foot. An obvious example is a situation in which the man feels the woman is abusing or neglecting the children, or has otherwise shown herself to be an unfit mother.

Some women, as I've pointed out, don't really want the responsibility of child care; but to avoid the social stigma attached to a woman's giving up her children, they'll seek joint custody. The man may actually do most if not all of the parenting. In one such case, the father made a home for the children, spent time with them, and took care of them. The mother, once she had her freedom, rarely even gave them a phone call; and when she did contact them, she almost invariably left them upset. The father, who originally accepted joint custody because he was afraid his wife would have the edge in a custody fight, finally decided to go for it.

Sometimes a man deliberately uses joint custody as a stepping stone toward sole custody. A switch from joint to sole custody may be easier to carry off than a complete change of custody and may not require as strong a showing of change of circumstances. (In some states, he'd have to show that the child was physically or emotionally endangered in order to get a full custody change within the first two years.) So, for example, if a father thinks the mother may want to move out of state with the children, he may seek joint custody so as to be in a better position to go for sole custody if she tries to carry out her plans.

To Sum Up

Joint custody is no magical solution. Making it work is a difficult challenge that takes a real effort on both sides. If you're contemplating joint custody, you should go into it with your eyes open. If you have joint custody and it's not working, you now know what your options are.

10

GETTING MORE OR LESS: CHILD SUPPORT, ALIMONY, VISITATION

Aside from custody changes, most modifications of a decree, agreement, or order fall into one of three categories: child support, alimony, or visitation. In chapter 7, I outlined general principles that apply to all these types of modifications. In this chapter, we'll look at each category in more detail.

Child Support Awards Are Often Grossly Inadequate

In most states, both parents are responsible for child support in proportion to their financial ability. In practice, this means that the noncustodial parent (usually the father) pays some portion of his income to the custodial parent (usually the mother), who is providing the remainder of the cost of the child's care.

While courts vary widely across the country in setting support figures, in general the amounts are unrealistically low. According to the latest census data, child support awards—even when actually paid—add up to only about 15 percent of the average custodial family's total income, which often is below poverty level. The average court-ordered payment is only about $200 a month, and under voluntary agreements it's not much more. To make matters worse, initially low support awards tend to stay at that level, making it impossible to keep pace with the rising costs of raising a growing child. According to economic studies cited by the National Organization of Women, a typical woman raising a 2-year-old and a 4-year-old until the age of 18 is entitled to a total of about $40,000, while her estimated expenses at today's costs will be more than $450,000.

The situation is exacerbated by the fact that even if she works full time, the average woman earns only 71 cents for every dollar earned by a man. Studies done in Colorado showed that licensed day care cost twice as much in 1983 as the average child support payment.

Yet many men justifiably feel that child support takes too big a bite out of their paychecks, leaving them barely enough to get by. Let's face it: most of the time, the chief breadwinner makes too little money to support two households. No matter how the court slices that paycheck, someone's going to be hurt.

Grounds for Modifying Child Support

Many people live for years with what they feel is an unfair and untenable situation, not realizing that support awards can be modified and are modified every day. In a modification suit, a court may look at the same factors that were considered in the original support award: primarily the child's needs and the parents' ability to pay. Changes in the child's needs may be due to a number of factors, such as an increase in the cost of living, a talent or disability that develops and needs nurture or special care, or simply the additional food, clothing, educational, and other expenses that normally occur as a child gets older.

If the income balance between the parents changes, the support award can too. For example, if at the time of divorce a noncustodial father was making twice as much money as the mother, and five years later he's earning four times as much as she is, the court may order him to increase support. If, on the other hand, her income surpasses his, she may find the support award reduced. A job promotion, a job loss, becoming disabled, inheriting a large estate, or any such circumstance can trigger a modification of child support. The court also may take into account general economic conditions, such as inflation or a plant closing, which affect large numbers of people.

Courts, then, consider both needs and resources in determining whether a modification is called for. The main thing to remember is that normally, for a modification to be granted, something must have substantially changed.

Modifying To Meet the Child Support Guidelines

Are you getting too little child support? Are you paying too much? How can you tell? In the past, many people who felt they had gotten a raw deal had no recourse unless they could show a change of circumstances. Now there are objective standards that can help you to determine whether your support payments measure up and to get them adjusted if they don't.

During the past 10 years, courts in many states have developed guidelines for child support, which have been written into the statute books. What used to be a matter of judicial discretion evolved into a rule of thumb and finally into a presumption with the force of law. In other words, a judge must order at least the amount of support indicated by the guidelines unless there's a good reason not to.

Under the 1984 federal Child Support Enforcement Amendments, all states were required to establish such guidelines, either by judicial, legislative, or administrative action. The guidelines accomplish two objectives: they establish some modicum of fairness and consistency in support awards, and they avoid the necessity for a full, time-consuming hearing in each case.

Lucy and Jim have been divorced for five years. Their support order was entered before their state adopted its guidelines. Jim's salary hasn't changed much, and neither have Lucy's expenses for their son, Barnaby. But when she read about the new support guidelines in the newspaper, she realized that she was getting a smaller percentage of Jim's income for Barnaby's support than she would have received had her order been entered today. Can she go to court and get more?

This issue came up in Illinois recently. Some courts were allowing modifications of old orders to meet the guidelines and some weren't. Finally the legislature stepped in and said, "We're going to give you a one-time right to modification without showing a change of circumstances, to get you up to the guidelines." The law doesn't say whether the noncustodial parent will be allowed a similar modification if (as may sometimes be true) he's paying more than the guidelines require. But my feeling is that as the courts become accustomed to applying the guidelines, they will tend to seriously consider modifications in either direction to bring the amount of previously ordered support in line.

So, if your divorce or separation is not recent, compare your support order with your state's guidelines. If there's a significant difference, you may want to ask a lawyer about your chances for modification.

Straight Versus Percentage Orders

A support award may be expressed either as a straight dollar amount or as a percentage of net (after-tax) income. In Illinois, for example, the guidelines call for a noncustodial parent to pay from 20 to 50 percent of net income, depending on the number of children. For example, if the noncustodial parent is netting $300 a week and has one child, the guidelines call for child support of $60 a week.

Does it make a difference whether the support order calls for $60 or for 20 percent of net income? It certainly does. For one thing, the enforcement system is computerized, and computers have trouble enforcing percentages. In order to monitor compliance, the noncustodial parent would have to send in a pay stub every week to verify that he was paying the correct amount.

For this reason, many courts have said that an award must be stated in dollars. If that wasn't initially done, it's ordinarily a good idea to get the order changed. Perhaps a man didn't have a steady income at the time of the divorce or support order, and the award had to be couched in a percentage. If and when his income stabilizes, that's the time to substitute a straight dollar figure.

Of course, a fixed dollar award won't keep up with changes in income. A man may be making a great deal more than he was at the time of the divorce yet still be paying the same monthly amount—now a much smaller percentage of his income. Nor will a fixed dollar amount keep up with the child's needs. In an inflationary period, a specified number of dollars buys less and less. For example, according to the U.S. Department of Agriculture, the minimum cost of food for a family of four with two school-aged children rose from $67.10 to $68.80 a week in the six months between December 1987 and June 1988—an increase equivalent to five percent a year. A regular cleaning in a dentist's office, which cost less than $10 in 1975, ran nearly $18 in 1985. College tuition more than doubled during the same 10-year period.

There are two ways to handle these problems: by modifying the award or by means of an automatic escalation clause.

Automatic Escalation Clauses

Some divorce agreements have periodic cost of living increases built in. (Such provisions are mandatory in Minnesota and New York.) These automatic escalation clauses, usually based on the consumer price index or some sort of percentage formula, are intended to avoid the necessity and the expense of going to court repeatedly for modifications. The burden is on the noncustodial parent to prove that he can't afford an increase, rather than on the custodial parent to ask for more.

Courts in some states have struck down escalation clauses that weren't clearly related to the parent's income or the child's needs. In general, courts tend to favor clauses tied to the consumer price index or some similar standard, even though some courts have held that inflation alone isn't enough of a change of circumstances to warrant a modification.

Personally, I'm a bit wary of escalation clauses. Anything automatic is unlikely to fit a particular family's needs. Linking increases in child support to the consumer price index may make sense for moderate income families but not for those in higher income brackets.

Automatic escalation is a simplistic, one-dimensional approach based on a single factor: the cost of living. Although it doesn't prevent either parent from asking for a modification based on changed circumstances, there's a tendency to be lulled into inaction—to live with the existing formula rather than go back to court.

Review Your Award Periodically

Especially if an award does not have an automatic escalation clause (and even if it does), it should be reviewed at least every three to four years. If a woman comes into my office and says, "I need more child support," the first question I ask her is, "When was the last time you received an increase?" If she tells me, "I think it's been five years," I don't have to go any further; I know she needs more.

What happens when the oldest child reaches the age of 18? That depends on the precise wording of the award. For example, let's say the wording is, "The husband shall pay to the wife $600 per month for the support of the three minor children." Contrast that with, "The husband shall pay to the wife for support of the three minor children the sum of $200 per month per child." The second award clearly provides for an automatic reduction when a child turns 18, without having to seek a modification; the first doesn't.

Is a Child the Absent Parent's Financial Partner?

If a divorced father wins the state lottery, should his children get a piece of the action? That question arose in a recent Illinois case, and the trial court said yes. The lucky father found his child support payments greatly increased. He appealed, arguing that the modified award had nothing to do with the child's actual needs. But the court of appeals said a trial court has discretion to order support commensurate with a parent's resources, even if that level of support exceeds the child's apparent needs. In other words, the court may consider the standard of living the child would have enjoyed had the marriage continued.

So, if an absent parent gets a windfall or enjoys a dramatic jump in income, the child may be able to share in that good fortune. But to what extent? Should the usual percentage guidelines apply? Some courts might hold that a child doesn't really need 20 percent of a $200,000 income.

The guidelines were developed for people who are barely getting by: there's a small pie to split up, and no matter how it's divided, it isn't enough. But in more sophisticated cases, the guidelines become less significant. Rather than a simple matter of percentages, it becomes a question of weighing the child's needs against the right to share in an absent parent's lifestyle.

Modifying Alimony

As I explained in chapter 7, alimony (or spousal maintenance) may or may not be modifiable, depending on how it was set up in the divorce decree. If maintenance wasn't waived or designated as nonmodifiable, it probably can be changed. Some maintenance orders have automatic escalation clauses.

As with child support, alimony awards and modifications generally are based on the woman's needs and the man's ability to pay (see Box 6 for a detailed listing of criteria). For simplicity's sake, I'll refer to the recipient of alimony as the woman and the payor as the man, although the reverse can be true.

The same considerations regarding straight versus percentage orders apply to alimony as to child support. If you don't trust your ex to live up to a percentage deal, you'd be wise to get your award translated into dollars. But if your ex is faithfully keeping the bargain on a percentage basis, you'd be foolish to upset the applecart.

When Is Rehabilitation Not Rehabilitation?

Courts now expect a woman, unless she's too old or physically frail or disabled, to "rehabilitate" herself. That is, she must become qualified for remunerative work and move toward self-support within a reasonable period of time. So even if a man is earning more money than he was at the time of the divorce, he

Box 6

Guidelines for Alimony

An increasing number of states have developed detailed guidelines for courts to take into consideration in awarding or modifying alimony. Criteria for an initial award may include some or all of the following, many of them taken from the model Uniform Marriage and Divorce Act of 1974:

•How long the couple were married.

•How old they are.

•Their physical and emotional health.

•Their respective educational levels, both at the time of the marriage and at the time of the divorce.

•How the property is to be distributed.

•A homemaker's contributions to her spouse's career and lifestyle.

•Her earning capacity (training, skills, work experience, length of time away from the job market, child care responsibilities, and time and expense needed to become qualified for appropriate employment).

•Whether (and how soon) she may be expected to maintain her own standard of living at a level comparable to that she enjoyed while married.

•Her ex's ability to meet her needs as well as his own needs and financial obligations.

•Any agreements they made on the subject before or during their marriage.

•The tax consequences to both parties.

Just as states vary in their criteria for an initial award of alimony, they also have different standards for determining whether it should be modified. A 1985 Alabama case, *Murphy v. Murphy,* outlined some common criteria, including:

•Has the paying party remarried?

•Has the recipient become employed?

•What are her needs and financial status?

•Is she now capable of supporting herself?

•Can her ex meet her financial needs?

•Are there dependent children?

•Was alimony originally agreed upon?

•Has there been a material change in the financial condition of either or both of the parties?

•What is their health, age, and education?

•What is their respective earning ability and prospect for future earnings?

•How long were they married?

•How much time has passed since the original award?

•Does the evidence of the particular case show any other relevant circumstances?

Some other common factors are:

•What does the decree say regarding modifications?

•Was the award for a specified number of years?

•Does state law require the recipient to attempt to "rehabilitate" herself?

may be able to get his maintenance obligation reduced rather than increased.

The definition of rehabilitation is key, especially in view of the trend toward reviewable maintenance. Let's say a woman has been given maintenance for four years, reviewable at the end of that period. During that time she has acquired a master's degree, her children have grown up and left the nest, yet she still hasn't found a job. Is she rehabilitated?

Before we can answer this question, we may need to look at some others. Has she tried to find employment? Has she tried hard enough? Is the field in which she chose to get her degree crowded with applicants? Low-paying?

I have a client who wanted to be an artist. She went to art school for four years and then had trouble finding work that paid more than a pittance. Could she claim that she had made a good faith effort at rehabilitation? Could the court say, "Too bad, we don't agree with your career choice?" Should her ex-husband, who was making $200,000 a year on the stock exchange, be able to wash his hands of his obligation to support her?

In this particular instance, the judge indicated that while she was entitled to pursue her art, it had been a seven-year marriage and her ex shouldn't be paying maintenance forever. We settled the case for enough money to give her a cushion while she found a more realistic way of supporting herself.

How Does Cohabitation Affect Alimony, and How Do Courts Define It?

If a woman takes a live-in lover, can her ex stop paying alimony? Generally yes; though in one Michigan case, a court of appeals held that the cohabitation would have to constitute a change of circumstances.

Defining cohabitation can be tricky, and the way a particular court defines it can make a big difference to your bankbook. Most states have held that living with someone who isn't your spouse isn't reason enough in and of itself to cut off or reduce alimony; merely taking a roommate of the same or opposite sex doesn't establish that you're cohabiting. Cohabitation generally is taken to mean that a couple are "residing together on a continuing, conjugal basis"—that is, living together as if they were husband and wife. Courts will often look to see whether a couple are "holding themselves out" as if they were married: for example, by having joint bank accounts or using the same last name.

The requirement that cohabitation be "continuing" is meant to exempt the occasional fling. If a woman stays overnight or for a weekend at her boyfriend's house, or even takes a two-week trip with him, she's probably safe. In fact, in one New York case, a liaison that continued on and off for 15 years was held not to excuse the woman's ex-husband from his maintenance obligation.

I had a client whose husband had agreed to pay alimony for six years. He had a home in Hawaii, where they had spent their winters while they were married. After the divorce, my client continued to visit Hawaii and became involved with a man she met there, staying at his villa for several weeks at a time. Her ex, who was still wintering in the islands, found out about the liaison and filed a petition to cut off her maintenance. The court refused after I pointed out that the woman was spending only a limited amount of time with her lover, that they were not holding themselves out as husband and wife, and that she was dating other men back home.

How Can a Woman Lose Possession of the House?

The issue of cohabitation sharpens when, as is common, the woman has been given exclusive possession of the family home. The way this sometimes works is that she has the right to live in the house with her children until the youngest child reaches age 18 or some other fixed date, at which time the home is to be sold and the proceeds divided between the ex-spouses. During the intervening years, each retains a financial interest in the home.

Often the mortgage is an old one, the payments are relatively low, and the mother's share of the equity at the time of the divorce would be insufficient to afford comparable or even adequate housing for herself and the children. The father may be willing to postpone realizing his portion of the equity in order to maintain family stability and avoid disturbing the children's lives. But if he finds out that his ex has taken a live-in lover, he may rebel: "I don't mind supporting her and the kids, but I don't want to support some other guy!"

Depending on the circumstances, it's possible to get such an arrangement changed, even though technically it's part of the property settlement, which normally isn't subject to modification. Courts have construed exclusive possession of the home to be a form of maintenance and thus modifiable.

In one case I had, the mother actually moved herself and her children out of the house and rented it out for income! My client, the father, objected. He wanted his family to have the use of the house; he did not want his ex-wife to be able to use it as an investment. I persuaded the court to order an immediate sale of the house on the basis of a change in circumstances: the fact that the ex-wife and children were no longer living there.

How Drastic Life Changes Affect Child Support and Alimony

Courts are accustomed to dealing with the usual changes of circumstances that prompt modifications (Johnny needs braces, his father gets a raise, his mother loses her job, and so on). But what if the change is a more drastic one?

Disability is one such change. In most states, if a child is disabled, the support order can be modified to continue the support obligation beyond the age of 18 and possibly for the child's entire lifetime. This is true whether the disability occurred before or after the order was entered.

A crippling illness of an ex-spouse or child may necessitate an increase in child support and/or maintenance, but the increase isn't likely to be granted unless the ex-mate has the means. I had a client in her twenties who developed multiple sclerosis and was confined to a wheelchair. Her ex had a low-paying job and couldn't come up with the kind of money her treatment required. Yet when she applied for public assistance, she was told that her ex-husband was obliged to support her. To get out of this catch-22, we had to get a court order showing that he couldn't pay for the treatment, so that she could get welfare benefits.

What if a man becomes disabled? Does that release him from his support or maintenance obligation? Not necessarily. If he's getting any kind of disability insurance or pension, his ex can claim a percentage of that.

If a man is drafted into the army, a court will most likely reduce his child support obligation. On the other hand, if a non-custodial parent inherits a fortune, his support obligation is very likely to be increased. In addition to the children's sharing in the estate, his ex-mate also may have a claim, particularly if the decree provided for a reservation of rights or reviewable maintenance.

Voluntary Changes of Circumstances

The examples I've just given deal with involuntary changes, whether for better or worse. What about significant changes that come about voluntarily?

Richard was a highly successful brain surgeon. Six months after his divorce, which had been of the knock-down-drag-out variety, he decided that he was burned out and wanted a complete change of lifestyle. He had always loved nature, so he moved to Colorado and went into business as a camping outfitter. The first year his income was one-fifth what it had been the year before, but he was happy. The only thing was, he couldn't make the hefty alimony payments that had been keyed to his former earnings. So he petitioned for a modification. The court said no.

Many times, when a person with an alimony or child support obligation voluntarily leaves a job (or a self-employed person decides to cut his own salary), courts will hold him to his original agreement even though he's now making less money, on the theory that the change was within his control. This is especially true when the change comes soon after the breakup, suggesting that the career move may have been vindictive. ("Why should I work my butt off for her?")

These are tough cases. Maybe a man who was making $300,000 a year in top management of a corporation really is sick of the rat race and wants to open a classical music store. Sometimes a person goes into a new venture in good faith and it simply fails. There are times when a court finds that a career change entailed a reasonable risk. But there's a difference between such a situation and one in which a person is laid off through no fault of his own, and most courts will treat these situations very differently.

Remarriage

Remarriage is a major, voluntary life change that can have a variety of ramifications. For example, Brian, immediately after his divorce, was living in a two-room apartment. He was paying unallocated support (a combination of child support and alimony) of $300 a month out of his salary of $800 to his ex-wife, Ann, for her and their two children. Three years later, Brian married a woman with five children and bought a ten-room home to accommodate his new family. The court, recognizing the additional dent his mortgage payments were making in his paycheck, adjusted the support payments to $250.

Brian was fortunate. Most courts would have said that establishing a new family was a voluntary choice, that his first responsibility was to his original children, and that the new dependents didn't constitute grounds for modification. But some courts will consider that factor, especially when a reasonable amount of time has passed.

Now let's take a look at the latest twist in Brian's case. The year after his remarriage, Ann also remarried (which means she's no longer entitled to alimony—a common provision in divorce decrees). Her new husband, Jack, is a wealthy financial consultant with three children of his own who attend private schools. Ann feels that her two youngsters should do the same.

Should Brian pay more child support because Ann's remarriage has exposed their children to a more expensive lifestyle? It's a subtle issue, and courts may go either way. Legally, a new husband like Jack has no obligation to help support his wife's children from a previous marriage. In practice, though, it's likely he will. The same sort of question arises when there are children born of a new marriage. If these "other" children can go to Europe for the summer, go to overnight summer camp, or attend private school, should the children of the first marriage be able to do the same?

Suppose a father marries a rich widow and moves in with her. A court can't order his new wife to support his children. But a judge may well find that because she's providing him with room and board, he has more disposable income left over that could be spent on the children.

Tactics in Monetary Modifications

As you know by now, in modifying child support or alimony, courts look at two factors: needs and ability to pay. It's relatively easy to prove that needs have increased. But unless you (the custodial parent) can also prove that your ex has increased income and can afford to meet those needs, you're likely to lose.

How do you find out? You can't expect your ex to volunteer that information. This is a real dilemma: you can't get access to your ex's tax returns unless you file a suit, but it's not advisable to file suit unless you're pretty sure you have a good case. Otherwise, you'll waste a lot of money on attorney's fees, and if the court finds that you filed a false pleading, you may be stuck with your ex's fees as well.

What you have to do is keep your eyes and ears open for indications of increased earnings. Often the children will be your best source of information: "Daddy bought a Cadillac and moved to a building with a doorman," or "Pop reads the racing forms every day. He won big last week," or "Mom says next summer she's going to take me to France." Tip-offs like that are signals that it's time to see your lawyer about a modification.

Proving the case can be a challenge. What if a man is moonlighting—delivering pizzas in the evening, or fixing neighbors' homes and taking payment in cash? What if he's self-employed and you suspect he's taking more money out of the till, but the records don't show what he actually earns? What if a woman is a waitress and makes her money in tips? You and your lawyer will have to look for direct or circumstantial evidence about your ex's lifestyle.

As always, it's wise to consider the possible downside before taking any action. What is the other party's reaction likely to be? What might you stand to lose? Are you happy with your decree overall? Are you paying less than the guidelines, or getting more? Is your visitation time unusually generous? Any time you petition for a change, you leave yourself open to a counterpetition. You may be better off to leave well enough alone.

Meeting the Visitation Guidelines

Visitation is the third main category of modifications, and here, too, courts have established guidelines. If you're the non-custodial parent and you're getting far less visitation time than a court would order today (say, one weekend a month), it's pretty easy to go in and get more time.

Parents often "modify" visitation informally to meet shifts in everyday routine. But a major or ongoing change should be written into your decree, order, or agreement.

One important reason for seeking to modify visitation exists if you have evidence that your ex is abusing your child. I'll discuss this sensitive issue in chapter 14.

If Your Ex Tries To Take Your Child Out of State

The worst fear of many a divorced father materializes when he finds out that his ex plans to move out of state with the children. Maybe she's getting married and her husband-to-be has been transferred. Or she herself may have gotten a new job miles from home. Or she may want to live closer to her family. Or maybe she's actually vindictive enough to do this just so her ex won't be able to see his children.

What can you do if this happens to you?

First of all, your decree should require that she seek the court's permission before she can move your child out of state. You must then be notified, and you can object on the grounds that you'd be losing your visitation rights.

Of course, in the United States, a citizen is free to move wherever he or she wishes. So a court can't tell your ex not to move. But if the court has jurisdiction over the child, it can tell her where the child may live. Thus if she insists on moving your child, and if the court determines that the move is not in the child's best interests, she may lose custody. The case will hinge largely on whether she has good reason for moving the child and whether there's a viable way to accommodate your visitation rights.

If infrequent fathering isn't to your taste, you may be able to nip your ex's move in the bud by beating her to the legal punch as soon as you get wind of her plans. As with harassment threats, a petition for an injunction against taking your child out of state may dissuade her from proceeding. If she insists on going through with the move, she'll have to file a counterpetition for removal; and, again, she'll have to prove that the move is in the child's best interests.

If you decide not to fight the move, or if the court allows it, your visitation rights will need to be modified. There are several points that will need to be discussed and settled. You'll need a new, viable visitation schedule. For example, you might take the child for eight weeks in summer and two weeks at Christmas and spring vacations, to make up for the loss of visitation during the school year. You also might agree on an equitable division of travel costs; one possibility is a cut in child support to compensate for your airfare when you come to see your child. All this represents a significant modification of your decree, and even if you and your ex agree, you should go back to your attorneys to make the changes.

How Do Courts Decide Whether a Child Should Be Moved?

Courts used to be fairly lenient about letting the custodial parent remove a child, but the trend now is to tighten up. Especially if the parents have joint custody, the courts will be reluctant to let one parent take off with the child.

A 1987 Illinois Supreme Court case, *In re Marriage of Eckert*, illustrates the delicate balancing act a court may go through. Here are the facts on which the court based its ruling:

Carol Eckert, who had custody of her seven-year-old son Matthew, was offered a position teaching nursing in Yuma, Arizona, and she petitioned for permission to remove Matthew to that state. The job, according to her petition, represented an advancement over her current position in Belleville, Illinois, and the dry climate would be good for Matthew's asthmatic half brother Bernie, Carol's son from a previous marriage. There also was evidence that Carol had been dating a doctor in Yuma, with some talk of marriage.

Carol's ex-husband, Mark Eckert, objected to the removal. Mark, according to the court-appointed psychologist, had been an excellent father. Despite considerable testimony that Carol had tried to interfere with visitation, Mark had never missed a visit with his son and was involved in all aspects of the boy's life—a relationship that (the psychologist stated) contributed to Matthew's good adjustment. Mark argued that Carol's contemplated move would irrevocably harm that relationship and would be traumatic for Matthew. He claimed that his ex-wife wanted to move for her own reasons and not for Matthew's benefit.

The trial court denied Carol's petition. The case made its way to the state Supreme Court, which reversed an Appellate Court ruling in Carol's favor and told her she could not move Matthew out of state. Pointing out that Carol had the burden of proving that the removal would be in her child's best interests, the high court upheld the trial court's view that she had not made a strong enough case.

While recognizing that a decision about the best interests of the child depends on the particular circumstances of each case, the court outlined several factors to be considered in evaluating a proposed move:

• The likelihood that the move will enhance the quality of life of the custodial parent and the children.

• The motives of the custodial parent in seeking the move. (Is it "merely a ruse intended to defeat or frustrate visitation"?)

• The motives of the noncustodial parent in resisting the child's removal.

• The effect on visitation rights of the noncustodial parent. (Can a "realistic and reasonable" new visitation schedule be established, and will the move impair the noncustodial parent's involvement with the child?)

Just what would be a "reasonable" visitation schedule would depend on the existing situation, the court made clear; and the degree to which the noncustodial parent had exercised his visitation rights would play an important part in the decision. When a parent like Mark had "assiduously" exercised those rights, the court expressed great reluctance to interfere with them "for frivolous or unpersuasive or inadequate reasons." Furthermore, the court pointed out, one of the aims of Illinois law regarding child custody (as in other states) is "to secure the maximum involvement and cooperation of both parents regarding the physical, mental, moral and emotional well-being of the children."

To Sum Up

Although the topics covered in this chapter are diverse and not necessarily related, the main point is that many aspects of a decree, order, or agreement can be changed. Don't assume, because a provision is in black and white, that it's unalterable. If you're dissatisfied with the way some provision of the document is working out, by all means review it and check with your attorney about the possibility of modifying it.

11

BACK TO SQUARE ONE

Up to now, we've been talking about how to enforce or modify a decree, order, or agreement. But there are certain circumstances in which a document can be nullified—that is, declared null and void. These circumstances generally constitute either (1) fraud, (2) coercion, or (3) incapacity or mental incompetence.

If you feel that your situation falls into one of these three categories, you might consider going for a nullification. But be aware that this is an extraordinary remedy, one that's not easy to obtain. You'll have to convince a judge that you were tricked or fraudulently induced to agree to a settlement, that you were forced or pressured, or that you weren't in condition to be responsible for your actions. In other words, you have to prove either that your ex did something to you that prevented you from entering into an agreement in full knowledge and of your own free will, or that there was something about you that caused you to be unable to do so.

Let's look at some examples involving each of these types of circumstances.

Fraud

Commonly it's the woman who cries "Fraud!" Her ex-husband may have hidden or undervalued some of his assets in order to obtain a more favorable property division, or falsified the books of his business to appear as though he was earning less.

I represented a woman whose husband was a lawyer. For purposes of the financial settlement, he stated that he had no unusual cases pending and no reason to expect a significant rise in income. Then, two weeks after the divorce, he settled a million-dollar case that had been pending for five years. In another case, a man valued some privately traded stock at $500,000; six months later he sold it for $10 million. His ex-wife, who had accepted a $150,000 settlement, found out about the stock deal after she heard through the grapevine that he was a major investor in a $50 million shopping center. She went back to court and got a new settlement in the millions.

Fraud can result in more than a revised financial settlement. In an Illinois case, a doctor who denied the existence of $67,000 in money market accounts was found guilty of criminal contempt. He was sentenced to do 13 weeks of community service at the county hospital and spend the weekends in jail.

Sometimes it's the man who's the victim. I represented a man whose wife inherited $500,000 but concealed it from both him and the court when she signed affidavits of her net worth. The husband agreed to give her most of the marital property, to pay alimony, and to foot the bills for the children's college education without any contribution from her—terms he certainly wouldn't have accepted had he known about her nest egg. Seven years later, he ran into her brother, who had always been a ne'er-do-well. The man was driving a Cadillac and wearing designer clothes. My client put two and two together. He did a little investigating and found out that his ex's uncle had died before the divorce, and she and her brother had come into the estate.

You may be wondering whether my client was able to raise this issue after seven years. The answer is, yes. Generally speaking, state statutes of limitations bar nullification more than two years after a divorce, but in most cases the statute of limitations begins to run when the fraud is discovered.

Nullifying the Terms or the Divorce

In the cases I've been discussing, what was actually nullified, as often is done, was not the divorce itself but the financial settlement. There are some very practical reasons for this. For example, the plaintiff may be remarried. Rather than undo the divorce, the judge vacates, or sets aside, the terms of the divorce and orders a new trial on the basis of the facts as they actually were. The result is something like a modification, but there's no need to show a change of circumstances because the original order was flawed by the circumstances surrounding its issuance.

In other instances, a plaintiff may seek to invalidate the divorce itself. A woman who had a terminal illness didn't want her husband to inherit her money, so she got a quick default divorce by falsely swearing that she didn't know where her husband was. After her death, he challenged the divorce, saying that he had had no knowledge of the proceedings and was therefore entitled to his share of the estate.

Divorce by Default

I've referred to default divorce earlier in this book. But you may be wondering how a divorce can be granted without one party's being present or even knowing about it. Here's how that might legitimately happen. A default judgment can be granted when one party fails to respond to notice of the trial. In most states, if you disappear and your wife doesn't know your whereabouts, she can sign an affidavit that you've been gone for a certain number of years and can't be found. Her lawyer can then serve notice on you by publication in the newspaper rather than by delivering the notice to you in person, as is normally required. After a reasonable interval, usually 30 to 45 days, if you don't appear, she can get a divorce by default.

The purpose of allowing notice by publication is so that the deserted party isn't left dangling indefinitely. If you've vanished without a trace, a default judgment based on such notice may well be the only way your wife can regain single status.

Suppose, however, that your wife really knows where you are all along. She lies to her lawyer, publishes the notice, and gets the decree. First thing you know, you're divorced! Based on your wife's fraudulent actions, you have grounds for nullification. You don't necessarily have to prove that your wife actually knew where you were if you can establish that she could have found you with reasonable effort. For example, you could prove that you're listed in the phone book, or you haven't changed jobs, or you have seen the children regularly.

As I said, if you really can't be found, a court can dissolve your marriage by default, upon publication of notice. But in such a case, the court would reserve the issues of alimony and child support. That's because, without personal service of notice, the court can have jurisdiction over the marriage but not over matters affecting the interests of the absent person.

One woman thought she had found a way around that. When she discovered that her husband was having an affair, she served him with notice of a divorce action. He took her to dinner, sent flowers, and promised to behave. She agreed to take him back and told him she was dropping the suit. Only she didn't. He, lulled into complacency, never filed a reply.

Meanwhile, the case went ahead, the court date arrived, and the man didn't appear. The woman testified that her husband was making $200,000 a year. Since he had been personally served but hadn't responded, the judge ordered alimony of $3,000 a month.

Next day the man stormed into my office and threw the decree on my desk. "This is ridiculous!" he sputtered. "We've been sleeping together for the past two months. All of a sudden I'm thrown out of my house and I'm saddled with a ton of alimony. What can I do?" Well, there was plenty he could do. With those facts, I was able to get a court to void the judgment on the basis of his wife's false assurances to him that she was withdrawing the suit.

Coercion

The second way that you may be able to invalidate your

decree is by offering evidence that you were forced, pressured, threatened, or abused. For example, if you agreed to un-favorable terms because your husband beat you into submis-sion, a court will almost certainly throw out the order.

Coercion needn't be physical. A woman named Judith came into my office a year after her divorce. Her husband, an attorney, had drawn up the agreement, and she had signed it without seeing a lawyer of her own. She had given away everything. She had waived alimony, let him have custody, and received virtual-ly none of the marital property.

"Why did you do such a thing?" I asked her.

Tearfully, she confessed that she had been sexually involved with a prominent politician. Her husband had caught them together, taken pictures, and threatened that if she didn't accept his terms, he'd send the photos to the newspapers and ruin her lover's political career. She had caved in.

Now the affair was over, the politician had been turned out of office for reasons having nothing to do with her, and she real-ized that she had sold herself down the river. She decided to come forward and tell her story—to try to get her children back and recover some of the marital property. The court agreed that the husband's actions constituted a clear case of emotional blackmail and vacated the order.

Incapacity

The third possible ground for nullification is that you were incapacitated, or not competent to enter into an agreement. That doesn't necessarily mean that you were mentally ill. It may mean that you were emotionally distraught, inebriated, overdosed with medication, under the influence of drugs, or for some other reason were unable to understand and take responsibility for what you agreed to.

A man named Joe came to see me, bewildered and somewhat incoherent, clutching a sheaf of divorce papers. He didn't remember signing them; but there was his signature, in black and white. What had happened was that he had been hospital-ized for a month in an alcoholic ward. Meanwhile his wife had gone to court and, while he was still in a stupor, had gotten him to sign the papers. The court held that Joe had been incompetent and vacated the decree.

Technical Grounds for Nullification

Occasionally there are technical reasons for nullification. It may turn out that the court that entered the judgment lacked jurisdiction to do so. State residency requirements vary and should be checked. In Pennsylvania, for example, a person filing for divorce must have lived in the state for six months. If you and your husband have lived there for only three months, but he states in his affidavit that he has been a resident for six months, the decree can later be overturned for lack of jurisdiction.

Or suppose you and your wife live in Arizona and you file for divorce there. Your mate, unhappy with the judge assigned to the case, goes across the border to Nevada (which has only a six-week residency requirement), spends six weeks at the casinos, files her own divorce action, and secures a decree. If you bring the prior pending action in Arizona to the attention of the Nevada court, the case will probably be reopened and the judgment vacated. (Incidentally, there's generally no statute of limitations for nullification based on a jurisdictional flaw.)

Another technical wrinkle: let's say a divorced man wants to marry again. But having been burned once, he's worried about the possibility of later being burdened with alimony for two ex-wives. So he insists that his bride-to-be sign a premarital agreement that if they divorce, she'll waive alimony.

The couple do divorce, and the woman waives alimony as she promised. Six months later, at a friend's suggestion, she consults an attorney, who informs her that premarital support waiver agreements are illegal in her state—something neither she nor her ex realized when they signed one.

Such waivers are banned in close to a dozen states, as contrary to public policy. In those states, since a waiver provision in a premarital agreement is illegal, it can't be allowed to govern a divorce settlement (and undoubtedly wouldn't have in our hypothetical case, if the court that granted the divorce had been aware of it). Any terms in the divorce agreement that are based on the illegal premarital waiver agreement are legally flawed and therefore null and void.

Nullifying Paternity

Is it possible to nullify a finding of paternity? Sometimes.

Before I tell you about one such case, I need to explain a few basic facts. A default judgment of paternity can't be entered without serving the alleged father with personal notice. Many times the man is served but doesn't show up, and the judgment is entered in his absence. The woman swears that she had sexual relations with this man on such-and-such date and the baby was born nine months later. The court declares the man the father and issues a support order. If he doesn't pay, his wages may be withheld.

In the case I referred to, my client was a successful, happily married doctor who had enjoyed a brief fling with a single woman. A year later, at his office, he was served with notice of a paternity suit.

"What's this all about?" he asked the woman. "I didn't even know you'd had a baby. How can you be sure it's mine?"

"It's yours, all right," she replied. "And if you fight me on this, I'm going to tell your wife. But don't worry—I don't want anything from you, and you don't have to bother to go to court. I'm never going to ask you for support; in fact, I don't ever want to see you again. I just want my baby to have a father's name."

My client took her at her word. He put the whole thing out of his mind until five years later, when he received notice that this woman was suing him for $25,000 in back child support.

What had happened was that, contrary to her promise, when the woman went to court she had secured not only a default paternity judgment but a child support order of $100 a week. At the time, she didn't need the money because she was living with another man. But she put the support order away in a safe place, and when her new boyfriend dumped her, she decided to go after my client.

I sought to nullify the paternity judgment, arguing that my client had never had his day in court—that he would have con-

tested the paternity suit were it not for this woman's false assurances that she would forgo child support. She, of course,
denied having said any such thing.

One of the factors that strongly influenced the court's
decision in my client's favor was that it had taken the woman
five years to do anything about enforcing the support order.
That circumstance, said the court, cast doubt on the woman's
motives and lent credence to my client's version of the story.

Even if a man was present at a paternity hearing and admitted to being the father, he may be able to get the finding in-
validated under certain circumstances. For example, consider
the following transcript:

Judge: Are you the father?

Defendant: Yes, I am.

If that was, in substance, the full extent of the interchange, the
man's lawyer could move for nullification. (I did that in a recent
case, and when the trial judge refused to nullify his own judgment, I got it reversed on appeal.) That's because in a paternity
case, which is a quasi-criminal action, a man must be apprised
of his rights—something like this:

Judge: Do you understand the nature of the charges against
you?

Defendant: Yes, I do.

Judge: Do you understand that you have the right to representation by an attorney?

Defendant: Yes, I do.

Judge: Do you understand that you have the right to take a
blood test that may establish the likelihood of paternity?

Defendant: Yes, I do.

Judge: Do you understand that by admitting paternity, you
will have an obligation to support this child until its maturity
and perhaps beyond?

Defendant: Yes, I do.

If, knowing all this, the man admitted paternity, it's unlikely
that he could later find grounds to avoid his responsibilities, unless he could prove that he was mentally incapacitated at the
time or had been coerced. But if he hadn't been told about his
rights to a lawyer or a blood test, or about his future support

obligation, he could probably have the judgment nullified.

Nullification Isn't Easy

Before closing this chapter, I want to reemphasize that nullification is an extraordinary remedy. A divorce decree, finding of paternity, or support order is based on sworn testimony. The burden of proof is on the person seeking to overturn it, and the proof needs to be very clear.

Coercion and incompetence are particularly hard to establish. And rightly so. Otherwise it would be too easy for people to back out of a signed agreement with the excuse that they had been upset, rushed, or pressured.

Unsuccessful attempts at nullification often follow a quickie divorce or last-minute settlement. I described one such situation in chapter 1, in which a couple went into court for a pretrial conference and ended up, unexpectedly, with a final agreement. This happens more often than you might think, especially in relatively simple cases.

Let's say your suit has been pending for months but you and your spouse have been traveling on business and haven't had much chance to talk out the issues, or your lawyers have been busy with other matters and haven't been able to get together. One day you find yourselves face-to-face in court on some sort of preliminary motion, say, for temporary support. The lawyers may sit down and say, "Why don't we just try to settle this whole thing?" Maybe the judge helps you and your mate reach a meeting of the minds. You have a quick pretrial hearing; the lawyers negotiate a deal right there at the courthouse, and almost before you know it, you're divorced.

Maybe the next day you wake up and say, "Hey, I think I got a bad deal." What can you do about it? Not much. What happened at the hearing, whether you realized it or not, is that the lawyers "proved up" the case; that is, a court reporter took down the terms as the lawyers read them aloud, and you and your mate both assented to them. If you try to get the agreement nullified, you'll be up against your own words, right there in cold black and white in the transcript:

Your Lawyer: Has anybody forced, coerced, or threatened you into entering into this agreement?

You: No.

Your Lawyer: Have you done so freely and voluntarily?

You: Yes, I have.

Your Lawyer: Are you satisfied with my representation of you?

You: Yes, I am.

You may have been sitting there saying "Yes, yes, yes" because you wanted to get the whole thing over with. Maybe you didn't really understand what was going on. You certainly didn't have much time to think. No matter; you were under oath, and it will be pretty hard to contravene your own sworn testimony.

Could you ever prevail in such a case? Yes, you could—under certain circumstances. You might be able to prove that your spouse had threatened to kill you, or to make sure that you never saw your children again, unless you agreed to his terms. You might have been heavily sedated with medication and your lawyer never asked you about that. You might have been under extreme pressure from your attorney to wind up the case ("You'd better take this settlement right now or I'm going to charge you double"). But without some such circumstance, you're probably stuck.

Many people after a divorce feel that they have been victimized, or that they acted hastily or foolishly. Unfair as it may seem, the fact that you got a raw deal, that you weren't thinking clearly, or that your lawyer was negligent or incompetent probably won't get you a nullification. Still, it may be worth talking to another lawyer to see whether there's some angle that can be used to attack the judgment.

Successful nullifications are fairly rare. But they do occur. If, after reading this chapter, you think you may have valid grounds, get together any evidence you may have to document your case and then call an attorney. You may just find yourself back at square one.

PART IV

Protecting Yourself and Your Loved Ones

12

WHO ELSE CAN GET INVOLVED? NEW SPOUSES, NEW LOVERS, GRANDPARENTS, AND OTHERS

For the most part this book deals with the two parties to a breakup and their children, if any. But other people can be drawn into legal battles that follow a divorce or the end of a non-marital relationship. As a couple move away from their original nuclear relationship, they develop a spreading web of connections with people who, in turn, have networks of their own. Inadvertently or intentionally, these new spouses and new lovers, as well as grandparents, siblings, friends, and even strangers may become involved as allies, adversaries, or innocent third parties whose own rights and interests may be affected.

Let's take a brief look at some of the ways these entanglements arise.

New Spouses Who Push for Custody

It's no surprise when a new wife presses for a reduction in her husband's alimony or child support obligation to his ex. What's not so well known is that it's often a new mate who—for competitive or other reasons—prods a noncustodial parent to seek custody of the children from the first marriage.

Recently a couple in their thirties came into my office. The man, a mild-mannered person, let the woman do most of the talking. She announced that her husband wanted to get custody of his five-year-old daughter away from his first wife, from whom he had been divorced for two years.

When I asked the man what grounds he might have for a custody change, the woman interrupted: "She's been living with a cocaine addict for at least a year. And that's not all; we have proof that this man is abusing the girl."

The father told me that until his remarriage six months before, he had felt he had no chance of obtaining custody because "the mother always gets the child."

"It's so unfair," his new wife interjected. "My husband is clearly the better parent! His ex just has a bigger mouth."

It was obvious to me that this man originally had lacked the stomach for a custody fight. His new wife was the one who was putting him up to it now. And, although officially not a party to the case, she continued to take a more active role than he did. She called me regularly to give me information and sent me a diary containing observations to back up the claim of abuse.

Even if a change of custody isn't the new spouse's own idea, his or her supportiveness can improve the chances for success by making the home environment seem more desirable. In a court's eyes, a new wife generally adds stability, especially if she's willing and able to stay home and care for the children. A new husband who's an ample breadwinner may make it possible for a mother to quit her outside job and devote herself to the children.

Custody Investigations

As a custody case continues, so does third-party involvement. Court-appointed investigators evaluate the child's prospective and existing households and all their members. A new spouse, as well as siblings and any other relatives or non-relatives who are living in the home, will be interviewed and observed. They may be required to undergo psychiatric testing.

The social worker doing the home study will probably ask questions about the new spouse's marital history—questions that may seem like an invasion of privacy. For example, a new husband might not be happy about having to explain why, if he's such a good prospect as a stepfather, he gave up custody of his own children and isn't on speaking terms with one of them. The investigators may even talk to his children and his ex, and they may be called to testify.

A New Spouse's Finances May Be an Open Book

A new spouse's financial privacy, too, may be at risk. If a father wants to pay less child support, the mother's new husband may think the issue is strictly between her and her ex. After all, a man has no legal obligation to support his wife's children from a previous marriage. But if he and his wife have filed joint income tax returns, her ex's lawyer can subpoena them to determine whether there has been any change in her income. When that happens, her new husband's income, too, becomes a matter of public record, whether he likes it or not.

The rules for what lawyers call **discovery** are quite broad. Lawyers are entitled to discover any information that might conceivably be relevant to a case, even though much of this information will end up not being admitted or even offered into evidence. Not only joint tax returns but joint bank accounts, deeds, mortgages, and other financial records are fair game for subpoena. If a couple have commingled any of their individual assets, the records become an open book, and both the man and woman may be forced to disclose information they would rather keep to themselves.

Let's look at an example. When Stephanie remarried, she and her 14-year-old son, Derek, moved in with her new husband,

Bob. After a couple of months, Bob told Stephanie that he was putting the house in her name to protect it from his business creditors.

Meanwhile, Stephanie's first husband, Mike, had fallen behind on child support. Instead of just filing an enforcement action, she figured she might as well try to get an increase, since she hadn't had one in five years. Now that Derek was in high school, the cost of his books and clothes, not to speak of his appetite, was growing by leaps and bounds.

After Stephanie filed her petition, Mike's lawyer, digging for evidence that she could handle Derek's increased needs on her own, subpoenaed all records about her finances, including any properties listed in her name. Thus when she filed suit to modify her support from Husband Number One, Stephanie unknowingly guaranteed that she would have to reveal her paper ownership of Husband Number Two's house—information he had intended to keep from his creditors.

Living with Trouble

Cohabitation is always risky, but there are special pitfalls when either party is divorced or has a child from a previous nonmarital liaison.

Alan, a longtime bachelor, was getting tired of playing the field and wanted to settle down. When he met Sarah, a divorcee with a 10-year-old boy, he figured she might be a good prospect. They got along well, and her son liked him. Pretty soon Alan was sleeping over at Sarah's place several nights a week. It seemed foolish for him to continue paying rent on his own apartment—he was hardly ever there—but he didn't feel quite ready to commit to marriage, so he suggested that he move in with Sarah. To his surprise and chagrin, she kept putting him off. He even began to wonder whether she was seeing someone else on the side.

When he finally pinned her down, it turned out that her reasons were extremely pragmatic. "If you move in," she explained, "I'll lose my alimony, and I won't be able to afford to pay the rent or even half of it. If that happens, are you prepared to pay the full amount? What's worse, if my ex, John, finds out you're living here, which he almost certainly will, I may lose custody of Tommy. John has always been terribly jealous and moralistic. He threatened to go to court the last time I got serious about someone, and he's bound to raise a fuss about my 'living in sin.'"

Not every divorced woman is practical and knowledgeable enough to anticipate such problems. Even if Sarah hadn't, Alan himself should have considered them. Did he feel willing and able to pay her rent if need be? Was he prepared to be a key figure in a custody fight or a suit for abatement of alimony? How would he feel if he were called in for a deposition and his financial records were subpoenaed to determine whether he was giving Sarah money? Just by moving in with her, he would have vastly increased his chances of becoming an inadvertent party to a messy lawsuit.

Just Dating Can Be Dangerous

Notice that I said "increased his chances." The fact is that the minute Alan became involved with Sarah, he became vulnerable to being drawn into her post-divorce legal problems. He wouldn't have to be living with her for John to claim that he was contributing to her support, or to harass or threaten either or both of them.

If Alan was married and was dating Sarah on the sly, his vulnerability would be even greater. Suppose her ex hired a private investigator to follow her and see who she was dating. The private eye would report that she was seeing a married man; and Sarah's ex, enraged that his son was being exposed to such goings-on, might file for custody and might even go so far as to get an injunction against Alan's spending time with Tommy. How long do you think Alan could keep his affair quiet under those circumstances?

If a custody suit went to court, it could be highly embarrassing to Alan, whose relationship with Sarah would become a key element of the case. He could be served with a subpoena at his place of work or at home, where his wife would most likely be present. He'd have to go to a lawyer's office and give a deposition under oath, with a court reporter taking down every word

Box 7

If You're Seeing a Divorced Person or Unwed Parent

•Go into the relationship with your eyes open.

•Think twice before moving in together.

•Keep your financial affairs strictly separate.

•Know what's in your partner's decree, agreement, or order.

•Ask about your partner's relationship with his or her ex.

•Be aware that you may become involved in litigation.

•See a lawyer for advice.

he said, and later he'd probably have to testify in court. His bank and employment records might be subpoenaed to prove that he was funneling money to Sarah in return for sexual favors. His employer might even be called as a witness.

In one case I handled, a wealthy suburban banker was keeping a mistress in a downtown penthouse apartment. His wife was blissfully unaware that her husband was playing around—until the mistress' ex decided to try to cut off her alimony. The ex, suspicious about where she was getting the money to maintain such a lavish lifestyle, subpoenaed her bank records and discovered a series of checks from her banker friend. The story hit the newspapers, and the banker lost his job as well as his marriage.

Little Slipups Can Come Back To Haunt You

No matter how careful you are, you're always vulnerable when you're involved with someone who has an ex in the wings. One of my clients left a suggestive message on his girlfriend's telephone answering machine. She neglected to erase the tape, and her ex-husband, who was nosing around while she got the kids ready for his visit, happened to play it back. Next thing my client knew, the tape was being used as evidence in a custody suit. "How can they do that?" he asked me. "Isn't it like a wiretap?" No, it isn't. No one tricked him into leaving that message; he did it of his own free will. When a person knowingly leaves a message on a recording device, it's no violation of privacy to bring the tape into court.

Another time, a divorced woman who was secretly dating a married man told her astrologer about their torrid relationship. The session with the astrologer was taped. Her ex got hold of the recording and used it to back up his claim that she was an unfit mother. Her lover, who hadn't known anything about the astrologer or the tape, was mortified when his wife found out that he had been subpoenaed as a witness in the case.

Grandparents Have Visitation Rights

Eight-year-old Benjie hasn't seen his grandmother Bess for two years. He remembers how she used to come over and bring him a box of freshly-baked cookies or a new toy. He loved going to her house and sitting on her lap while they looked through family pictures. It was fun to search for treasures, like baseball cards his father used to play with, hidden away in the closet of Dad's old room. After Benjie's mother and father got divorced, Grandma Bess continued to come around for a while, and her visits always helped calm him when he was worried or tense.

One day Benjie's mother told him that a new Daddy was coming to live with them, and a new brother and sister too. After that, Grandma's visits stopped. When Benjie asked his mother why, she replied that Grandma was too busy to visit him anymore, and besides, wasn't it nice that now he had a whole new family?

What Benjie's mother didn't tell him was that after her remarriage she had forbidden her former mother-in-law to see him. Her ex had given up his own visitation rights in return for abatement of child support. "Good riddance," thought Benjie's mother; she wanted to start fresh, to have nothing to do with her former husband or any member of his family. Grandma Bess, as heartbroken as Benjie, felt helpless to do anything.

Grandma Bess was wrong. In all likelihood, if she had consulted a lawyer she would have found out that there was plenty she could do.

Grandparents' rights are among the hottest topics in family law today. It's not unusual for paternal grandparents like Grandma Bess to find themselves out in the cold after a divorce. A woman may be perfectly happy to have her own parents around, but not her ex's.

Under the common law, she was within her rights; grandparent visitation against the wishes of the custodial parent was prohibited. But in the past few years, that principle has come under attack. Grandparents excluded from their grandchildren's lives have organized pressure groups that have lobbied for legislation. It's now generally recognized that continuing ties with loving grandparents are important to children's development—that children are hurt when they are kept from seeing grandparents and other close relatives.

Today virtually every state has a statute giving grandparents some sort of rights concerning visitation with their grandchildren after the parents' divorce, and in some states these rights extend to siblings and others. The statutes and their judicial interpretations vary, so grandparents who aren't being allowed to see their grandchild should check with a lawyer.

One caution: "visitation rights" aren't automatic. What the law gives grandparents is the right to petition a court to issue an order allowing them to see their grandchild. A key question the judge will consider is what kind of relationship they had with the child before their visits were cut off. If that relationship was a strong and loving one, the court is more likely to find that continuing to see the grandparents is in the best interests of the child. And that, as you know by now, is the bottom line in matters involving children.

On the other hand, a good prior relationship with the child won't guarantee a grandparent's winning visitation rights. The court may find, for example, that the visits are likely to arouse family tensions that would upset the child.

Incidentally, this is one situation in which the divorce decree is usually of no help. It's very rare that a decree provides for grandparent visitation. The issue almost always comes up afterward, when visitation is denied. Possibly one result of all the consciousness-raising grandparents have done will be that more couples will consider their parents' rights in drawing up future divorce agreements.

What happens to grandparents' visitation if a child is adopted by a stepparent? Courts have gone different ways. In some states, if a custodial mother's new husband adopts her children, the natural father loses all rights, and so do his parents and other family members. But in Iowa and North Carolina, among others, the grandparents' rights have been upheld. (Of course, if an unmarried woman or both natural parents give up a child for adoption, the natural grandparents normally lose any claim.)

Are There Reasons for Grandparents Not To Seek Visitation?

Some grandparents, though devastated by the denial of access to their grandchild, do nothing for fear that a court fight will upset the child. But such self-sacrifice is rarely necessary. A good lawyer with a statute in his pocket can often resolve the matter amicably through negotiations.

In *Hearts and Dollars*, I told of a father who made a private deal with his ex-wife after their divorce: he would stay away from the children if she would forgo child support. His parents, however, continued to see the children until their mother remarried and her new husband objected. When the grandparents came to see me, they were furious and seemed determined to press their case. And, given their long-standing relationship with the children, I felt pretty sure we could win.

But I also felt duty-bound to point out one possible hitch: because their son's deal with his ex had never been formalized (something I've warned about throughout this book!), if the case went to court he could be dragged in and forced to pay a huge amount of back support for the years before her remarriage.

The grandparents were faced with an agonizing dilemma: was seeing their grandchildren worth risking their son's solvency? My advice was to go ahead. If the child support issue came up, their son and his ex could negotiate a separate settlement. But if my clients didn't reestablish their relationship with their grandchildren, the opportunity might be lost forever.

So, if you're a grandparent who has been denied visitation, don't deprive yourself of the chance to watch your grandchildren grow up. And don't waste any time—those kids aren't getting any younger, and neither are you. Besides, if you do end up in court, the continuity of the relationship will be an important factor in the judge's decision. Every day that goes by with no contact lessens your chances of seeing your grandchildren again.

When Grandparents Act as Parents

Cases involving grandparents often arise when the parents are teenagers who have brought the baby home to live with the folks. Unwed mothers or young couples who are still in school or working as cashiers at the local supermarket usually can't swing a place of their own. If the mother's parents, for example, are paying the child's bills, they may seek child support from the father. (Statutes provide that whoever is actually paying for a child's care is entitled to reimbursement from the parents.)

In some cases, when grandparents are actually the ones raising the child, they decide to seek custody. What are their chances of getting it? Pretty good, especially if the parent or parents can be shown to be unfit.

An abused or neglected child doesn't have to be living with the grandparents for them to get custody. In one case, I helped a couple get custody of their five-year-old grandson over the objections of their drug-dazed daughter, who frequently left him alone for hours in the backyard or let him wander in an alley. This was an easy case; the girl was disheveled and practically incoherent, while the grandparents, in their late forties, were clean-cut and vigorous. But even if the grandparents had been in their sixties, the decision probably would have gone the same way.

In another case, grandparents teamed up with their teenaged son in a custody suit. He was in no position to take on the responsibility for childraising, whereas his parents could offer the child a stable home. So they agreed to become parties to the suit in order to help their son get his child away from an unfit mother.

Grandparent custody cases generally aren't as adversarial as those between ex-spouses. Usually the grandparents are interested mainly in protecting the child's welfare. If their son or daughter gets counseling or demonstrates the ability to care for the child, the grandparents are often more than willing to turn over custody.

Friends and Strangers Can Get Custody

Most state statutes provide that any person with physical possession of a child—even an unrelated party—may seek custody. A typical scenario might go like this: Nancy, a 16-year-old unwed mother, leaves her baby with her friend, Lana, while she goes to a drug rehabilitation center. "I'll be back soon," she assures Lana. "I just need a couple of days to get my head on straight."

A month later, Lana gets a letter with a distant postmark: "I'm doing better, but I haven't quite gotten my act together. Do you mind keeping the baby for a couple of months? Love, Nancy."

By that time, Lana has become attached to the baby. She goes to court and gets a temporary custody order. Six months later, Nancy shows up at Lana's door asking for her child. Lana refuses to surrender the infant.

"Some friend," Nancy shrieks. "You said you'd do me a favor, and now you're trying to take my baby away from me."

For Nancy to get her baby back, she'll have to convince the court that such a step is in the child's best interests—a proposition she'll have a hard time proving in light of her previous actions.

To Sum Up

Many times someone other than the original parties to a divorce or unwed relationship becomes involved in the legal aftermath, either voluntarily or involuntarily. Issues of custody, child support, alimony, and visitation all may involve third parties who may or may not be related to the former couple and their children. New spouses, new lovers, grandparents, and others need to be aware of their rights and their vulnerability when their lives are intertwined with someone whose previous marriage or relationship has broken up.

Two kinds of cases in which third parties, as well as the parents, sometimes play a part are those concerning child abuse and kidnapping, which I'll discuss in the next two chapters.

13

DON'T LET YOUR CHILD BE A VICTIM: CHILD ABUSE AND NEGLECT

When six-year-old Mark came home from his weekly visit with his father, he had fresh bruises on his arm. He told his mother that he had "bumped into something." She wordered about the incident but soon dismissed it from her mind. The following week, though, when she discovered a large crimson welt on his back, she became alarmed. After persistent questioning, she finally got Mark to admit that "Daddy gave me the strap because I was bad."

"He'll never do that to you again," she promised the weeping boy. And the next day she filed a petition to suspend her ex-husband's visitation.

Child abuse—physical, emotional, and sexual—is being raised more and more frequently as an issue in custody and visitation disputes, both before and after divorce or the breakup of an unwed relationship. (In Illinois, for example, out of 41,000

179

reports of sexual and physical abuse to the Department of Children and Family Services during the year that ended in June 1986, about 2,000, or 5 percent, were made in the context of custody battles.) Whether the charges are substantiated or not—in some cases they are used as tactical leverage—the child caught in the middle is a victim.

Some Facts About Abuse and Neglect

According to the National Committee for the Prevention of Child Abuse, the number of cases of child abuse and neglect reported to social-service agencies has been growing by about 10 percent a year since the mid-1970s. The most recent reports show that more than two million youngsters nationwide—infants to 17-year-olds—are victims of abuse and neglect; more than 11 percent of these cases involve sexual abuse. An estimated 5,000 youngsters a year die as a result of parental abuse and neglect. Since not all cases are reported, the actual extent of the problem is undoubtedly much greater.

Broadly defined, abuse is an act that harms a child, like kicking, scalding, or intimidating. Neglect is failure to provide a child with needed nurture (food, clothing, shelter, medical care, or emotional sustenance).

It's difficult for many people to understand why an adult, especially a parent, would harm a child. Psychological studies have shown that abusers and neglecters often were themselves abused or neglected as children. The idea that abuse is limited to the lower socioeconomic classes is a myth; it occurs at all economic and social levels, though privileged families usually can hide it more easily.

Studies show that abusers (who, except for sexual abusers, usually are mothers) may be under great emotional stress and may gain a sense of control over their own lives by flaunting their power over their children. Typically they don't display the normal human reactions of sympathy and concern; they respond to childish behavior with anger, hostility, and violence. Instead of picking up and comforting a helpless, crying infant, they may beat the child into silence. Often they feel revulsion and shame about their behavior but can't stop themselves.

Neglecters, on the other hand, tend to be emotionally withdrawn, irresponsible, and indifferent. Whereas abusive parents are passionately involved with their children in a negative, destructive way, neglectful parents pay little or no attention to them and may even wish the child had never been born.

Sometimes the line between abuse and neglect can be a narrow one. (So can the distinction between abuse and normal physical punishment; in fact, some child advocates argue that any form of physical punishment is abusive.) In one case I know of, a neighbor called the police one cold winter night to report that she had found two little girls, seven and nine years old, shivering on the stoop of the house next door. Their divorced father, with whom they were visiting, had locked them out. This might have been a case of neglect. But upon investigation, it came out that the man, who was between jobs and behind in his child support, frequently became enraged and shoved his daughters; once he had pushed the nine-year-old so hard that she hit her head on the kitchen counter and required stitches. Another time, in summer, he had taken the fair-skinned girls out in a boat for hours, unprotected from the hot sun, and brought them home blistered and crying—another instance of hostile "neglect."

One tip-off to the existence of abuse or neglect by a custodial parent may be that parent's unwillingness to let the other parent, the grandparents, or other concerned persons see the child. In one such case, a 15-year-old unwed mother brought home her infant son to live with her parents. Three years later, she took her child and moved in with her boyfriend. After that, the young mother refused to have anything more to do with her parents. When they called and asked to see their grandson, she got an unlisted phone number. At first the grandparents were baffled by their daughter's behavior. Why would she suddenly cut off all contact? Eventually they discovered that their daughter and her boyfriend were abusing the child.

Sexual Abuse—The Syndrome and Its Signs

Sexual abuse has been called "the silent plague." It has been estimated that one girl out of every four and one boy out of every seven is sexually abused at some time before the eighteenth birthday.

In an estimated 85 percent of sexual abuse cases, the abuser is someone the child knows, usually a male—a father, an older brother, an uncle, a neighbor, a teacher, or a friend of the family. Given the opportunity for frequent, intimate contact, psychologists say, a habitual pattern of behavior develops gradually between the older person and the child. Sexual abuse by a parent may be a long-standing family secret in which the other parent has been an unconscious coconspirator, looking the other way, not wanting to know. The child is often reluctant to reveal what's going on. Fear of the abuser blends with love and guilt—the feeling that somehow it's the child who's at fault.

Studies show that abuse may begin or surface during or after a breakup for a number of reasons, including family instability, stress and anxiety, and an increased sense of vulnerability. A single parent may seek to make up for the loss of adult caring and affection by getting it from a child in inappropriate ways. A child who was previously afraid to reveal abuse may be emboldened by separation from the abusing parent and by a closer, more trusting relationship with the other parent. Or disclosure may be spurred by the child's being forced to spend more time alone with an abusive parent who has custody or frequent visitation. On the other hand, in a divided family, if one parent is abusing the child it may be difficult for the other parent to find out and verify what's going on.

Both custodial and noncustodial parents should be alert to possible signs of sexual abuse. They need to tune in to subtle signals from children who may not be willing or able to put into words what's bothering them. Experts warn that if a child begins to have trouble going to sleep, suddenly loses appetite or starts eating voraciously, develops new fears, exhibits infantile behavior, refuses to go to a familiar place or to be with a certain person, or turns against a parent, sexual abuse may be the explanation.

Psychologists advise that if you find out your child has been sexually abused, the most important thing to do is to blame the perpetrator, not the child. Make clear that you'll do all you can to prevent the abuse from happening again.

Protecting a Child from Abuse and Neglect

What can you do to protect a child from abuse (sexual or nonsexual) and neglect? A network of organizations in various states have 24-hour hotlines and can offer moral support or refer you to governmental and private agencies; the National Coalition Against Domestic Violence in Washington, D.C., can furnish the phone number of the hotline in your state.

But to deal effectively with the problem, you'd be wise to see a lawyer—and the sooner the better. By taking quick action, you can prevent the situation from recurring or worsening. If you believe your ex-husband abused your child last Saturday, for example, you certainly don't want to let your child go with him next Saturday.

One immediate measure you can take is to seek an order of protection. (See Box 2, chapter 3. This also is a wise move if your ex is harassing or abusing *you;* often the two kinds of abuse go hand in hand.) If the alleged abuser harms, threatens, or harasses the person or persons named in the order, he or she will be in contempt of court and can be fined or possibly jailed. The order of protection can provide for custody, visitation, living arrangements, and other temporary modifications.

I had a case in which a divorced father, during his visitation periods, fed his three-year-old son nothing all day but candy and Kool-Aid and took him out in subzero weather without mittens. He also made a habit of calling his ex-wife at all hours. It seemed clear that this man (who had never taken much interest in the child before the divorce) was trying to get back at his ex for leaving him, and one way he chose to harass her was by neglecting the child. I obtained an order of protection for her and the boy. One night, while high on drugs, the man beat down his ex-wife's door and threatened to kill her. She scooped up her son and ran to a neighbor's house. Her ex-husband spent two months in jail for violating the order of protection.

Modifying Custody or Visitation: Civil Proceedings

In the case I just described, in addition to securing the order of protection, I successfully petitioned the domestic relations court to suspend the father's visitation rights. It's common sense that a parent who is using visitation as an opportunity to abuse or neglect a child shouldn't be given continued access to the child, or at most should be allowed supervised visitation. If, on the other hand, it's the custodial parent who apparently is abusing or neglecting the child, the other parent or some other concerned adult can seek a change of custody.

The best chance for modification of either visitation or custody is to show that the abuse or neglect developed after the original order was entered, thus constituting a change of circumstances. If you claim that this sort of thing was going on all along, the court will ask, "Why didn't you bring this up the first time?" And if you did charge abuse or neglect originally but your ex was awarded custody or visitation anyway, the court may say, "That issue has already been adjudicated." So, although a court will listen to such allegations at any time, it's best to rely on new rather than old information.

Quasi-Criminal Proceedings

Some abuse and neglect cases, rather than being adjudicated through civil suits as I've just described, are handled as quasi-criminal actions in juvenile or family court. If a report of abuse or neglect has been made to a state agency, there's no choice but to pursue the matter through the state's juvenile justice system.

A telephone call from a parent, relative, neighbor, doctor, a child's school, or even an anonymous person can set in motion a police investigation and a temporary or permanent change of custody or loss of visitation rights. The state, because of its interest in protecting children, can step in and, if the facts appear to warrant it, can take an allegedly abused or neglected child away from a parent. The public prosecutor may press charges, and the abuser, if found guilty, may be fined or jailed. The last stage of the proceedings is a final adjudication as to custody, which, as always, will be based on the best interests of the child.

State investigators and prosecutors often have heavy caseloads, so it's a good idea to take an active role in your case. Keep in frequent touch with the investigator. If you have the means, you can also hire a private attorney to represent you regarding custody or visitation.

Once the state's juvenile justice system takes over, it preempts any previously pending civil action. To illustrate how this can happen, let's look at a rather complex case I handled. An unwed couple had a baby boy and then separated. The father became alarmed when he found out that the mother was breast-feeding the infant while on alcohol and drugs, and the baby was showing definite signs of addiction. The father persuaded the mother to let him take care of the baby while she went to a drug treatment center. When she failed to get her drug problem under control, he came to us to file for custody.

During the court-ordered investigation (which was to include a home study and medical examinations of the mother and the child), the mother was given temporary custody provided she stayed drug-free. We didn't believe she could do it, and she didn't. Before the investigation even got under way, police (acting on a call from a neighbor) found her unconscious on the street. The baby was sitting next to her in a daze.

The police turned the baby over to the state's Department of Children and Family Services, and the prosecutor brought charges of abuse and neglect against the mother in juvenile court. When the father heard what had happened, we went into juvenile court on an emergency petition and obtained temporary custody. We filed in juvenile court because the state's action had superseded the pending suit in domestic relations court.

A new, more intensive investigation began in juvenile court. Meanwhile the mother was given another chance to straighten out, and again she failed, forfeiting any chance of getting the child back. Our client ended up with permanent custody.

How Common Are False Allegations of Abuse?

A respected financial analyst was accused of sexually molesting his three-year-old daughter. His ex-wife, angry about his leaving her for another woman, convinced the court to suspend visitation by offering in evidence a taped interview of the carefully-coached child backing up her story. The father, who vehemently maintained his innocence, was heartbroken but helpless.

In recent years, charges of abuse, particularly sexual abuse, have become potent weapons in custody and visitation disputes. Often the charges are all too true. But sometimes they are not.

The accused parent isn't the only victim in such a case. A false charge of abuse also causes trauma to the child, who may be a pawn in the hands of an embittered or emotionally disturbed adult and who will almost certainly be torn between attachments and loyalties to both warring parents.

Sometimes siblings are drawn in. I had a case in which a 16-year-old boy was accused of having sex with his 14-year-old stepsister. The girl had told her father that the boy had kissed her, and the father had stretched the story to bolster his claim that living in the mother's household was endangering the child. In another case, a retarded child allegedly had made sexual advances to his younger stepbrother. In both these cases, the court, after thorough investigation, found no merit to the charges, but the finding couldn't erase the trauma to all the youngsters involved.

How widespread are such false allegations? According to the National Committee for the Prevention of Child Abuse, about half of all reports of sexual abuse turn out to be unfounded. But that doesn't necessarily mean no abuse took place; often there's simply insufficient evidence to prove it.

Research suggests that false reports of abuse are only rarely intentional, self-serving, or vindictive. More often, "false" allegations arise from legitimate parental suspicions that prove, upon investigation, to lack substance. A girl may show a vaginal irritation after a visit with the father. The mother may report it as a possible sign of abuse, but it may turn out to have had some other cause. Nevertheless, the mother's initial suspicion was reasonable.

The largest study to date, of 576 sexual abuse reports handled by the Department of Social Services in Denver in 1983, found that nearly one-fourth had insufficient information to make a determination. Of the rest, 70 percent turned out to be reliable reports, 22 percent were reasonable but unsubstantiated suspicions, and only 8 percent (6 percent reported by adults and 2 percent by children) appeared to be fictitious. A significant proportion of these, as in several smaller clinical samples, arose in the context of custody and visitation disputes.

Certain features of postmarital family life tend to feed suspicions of abuse. Distrust of an ex, competition for the loyalty of the child, or genuine concern about sleeping arrangements and other aspects of the child's welfare may lead to misinterpretation or exaggeration of signs and symptoms. Emotional disturbance or stress may give a parent a distorted idea of what's going on when the child is with the other parent. Thus we can't necessarily equate "fictitious" with "malicious."

Get the Child To a Doctor Right Away

Obviously, an immediate physical examination can be a key to establishing whether or not abuse has occurred. Yet it's amazing how often the person discovering signs of abuse fails to get the child to a doctor.

In one case, now being appealed, a couple sought custody of their 12-year-old grandson, claiming that he had been physically abused by their son, the child's father. The boy, a product of a teenage marriage, had, as an infant, been sexually abused by his mother. Her parental rights had been completely terminated—a drastic and highly unusual remedy. Since then, the child and his father had been living in the home of the father's parents until three months before the couple came to see me, when father and son had moved into their own place.

After that, the family relationship had deteriorated dramatically. The boy's father seemed intent on keeping grandparents and grandchild apart. Finally the boy had been allowed to visit the grandmother on her birthday. As soon as he arrived, he took her aside and said, "Grandma, I want to show you something." What he showed her was not a birthday present but the marks of a belt buckle on his backside.

When the case went to trial, the boy and the grandparents testified to the abuse. But there was no medical report to back up their story, and the court held that the evidence of abuse was insufficient to allow the grandparents to challenge their son's custody. The judge felt that the testimony was self-serving; grandparents and grandson wanted to live together again, and there was no objective proof of what they said.

Will Your Child Have To Testify?

Abuse cases are tricky to handle because decisions about everything from whether to get medical documentation to whether the child should testify involve not simply the best strategy for winning the case but what's best for the child.

The emotional trauma to a child who has been abused seldom ends with the abuse itself; usually there are long-lasting psychological repercussions. Confronting the abuser in court and reliving the experience may further traumatize the child. Fear, guilt about the child's own imagined responsibility for the abuse, and attachment to the accused parent render some children unwilling or unable to testify. Concern for the child's welfare may keep the victim off the witness stand but also may result in letting an abuser off the hook and enabling him or her to resume contact with the child.

For this reason, a panel appointed by the U.S. Attorney General in 1984 recommended that children's testimony in abuse cases be presented on videotape. But that way the judge is denied the opportunity to observe and question the child, either on the stand or in chambers (where the child doesn't have to face the alleged abuser) and to form a direct impression of the child's credibility—which, especially in the absence of medical evidence, can be the crux of the case.

Appointment of a guardian ad litem can help to minimize

psychological stress on a victimized child. The guardian ad litem can help prepare the child for court appearances and keep other interrogations to a minimum. (Even if the child doesn't testify, he or she may be questioned by mediators, investigators, counselors, police, and prosecutors.) The guardian ad litem and/or a court-appointed psychiatrist may also recommend an appropriate plan for custody and visitation and for treatment of the child and the family.

How Reliable Is a Young Child's Testimony?

Research shows that adults tend to be skeptical of what young children say in court, particularly when it concerns alleged sexual abuse by a family member. In one 1983 study, fewer than 50 percent of psychologists, lawyers, and potential jurors felt they could give credence to an eight-year-old's testimony. A recent study at Yale University found that jurors' prior expectations about the reliability of a six-year-old's testimony are likely to color their assessment of what a particular child says and thus to influence the verdict in a sexual assault case.

Generally speaking, children are better witnesses than they are sometimes given credit for. Some research shows that even children as young as six can make as accurate reports as adults do. They can remember as well or better, they can distinguish between reality and fantasy, and they are no more suggestible. On the other hand, they tend to leave out details; and as time passes, they may become less willing to talk about an upsetting incident. If they were severely traumatized, they may be confused about such specifics as when or where the event occurred.

According to Dr. Arthur H. Green, medical director of the Family Center at New York's Presbyterian Hospital, it's common for a frightened, anxious child to deny incest, but it's rare for a child to make up such a story. Dr. Green, writing in the *Journal of the American Academy of Child Psychiatry*, said that when a child does make a false disclosure against a parent, it may be because the child is angry (perhaps for being punished), or the report may be based on a young child's sexual fantasies. Or a child may corroborate a mother's accusations for fear of losing her love and approval. The charge may have just enough of a kernel of truth to be believable; if a father acts a bit overaffectionate with his daughter, the mother may build up the incident by repeated reminders until the child believes that abuse actually occurred.

Other researchers suggest that a child may act out sexual behavior indicative of abuse because that kind of behavior gets adult attention. It's also possible for an investigator to unwittingly encourage a false report through leading questions.

Sorting Out the Truth

Courts often rely on psychiatrists, social workers, and other mental health professionals to help them get at the truth. Usually each side brings in its own experts who examine the child, and sometimes the court also appoints "neutral" experts.

Psychiatrists may test both the child and the parents, take a detailed history, and observe the child's behavior with each parent. For example, do the child's eyes constantly travel to the mother, as if checking with her while telling about abuse by the father? Does the child appear afraid to tell the story in the father's presence? (The former, according to some experts, would indicate a false account, the latter a true one.) The psychiatrist must be careful to make the child feel safe, to establish a sense of trust, and to protect the child from further trauma.

Sometimes it's not the existence of abuse but the identity of the abuser that's at issue. The use of both male and female examiners can help lay blame. If the child freezes up when examined by a man but is more relaxed when examined by a woman, the abuser was probably a male.

Once I represented a mother whose four-year-old son was a victim of sexual abuse. My client accused her ex-husband; he accused her father (the boy's maternal grandfather). Each party had a reputable psychiatrist to back up his or her claim, and each of these experts had interviewed and tested the child. I won the case when a third, court-appointed psychiatrist did additional testing that incriminated the boy's father. The point is that it can be very difficult to make such a determination on the basis of evidence given by a young child. In my experience, it generally takes a highly trained, highly competent professional to elicit consistent information from a child who may have been abused by a family member.

A growing body of professional literature provides guidelines for weighing a child's credibility. Fictitious reports generally lack detail; the child is likely to tell the story with little emotion and to use language inappropriate to his or her age. But researchers point out that such guidelines must be followed with caution. Because genuine victims of incest are usually reluctant to reveal it, they tend to do so haltingly, often contradicting themselves, whereas a child telling a fictitious tale may offer details readily.

SVA: A Promising Procedure

Statement Validity Analysis (SVA) is a method of interviewing allegedly abused children and assessing their credibility. It has been used internationally with some success.

The interviewer first establishes rapport by asking the child neutral questions like where the child goes to school. The child is asked to freely recall the incident in question without interruption, and then to repeat the story. Next the interviewer asks specific clarifying questions ("In what room did that happen?"). As is often done in abuse cases, a very young child may be helped to describe what occurred by the use of such props as anatomically correct dolls, a doll house with furniture, drawings, and clay figures. Finally the interviewer does a "suggestibility check," asking a few leading questions to see how susceptible to suggestion the child is. The child's statement, along with any accompanying evidence such as a medical report, is evaluated according to a detailed set of criteria of credibility and validity.

The interview is videotaped. This serves several purposes. It allows the interviewer to concentrate on asking questions rather than having to take extensive notes or rely on memory. It permits independent assessment by several observers while lessening the need for repeated questioning of the child, which can not only be upsetting but can elicit contradictory accounts. (Research shows that repeated questioning of young children reduces, rather than serving as a check on, their accuracy.) The

videotape may also be used in court as a supplement to, or substitute for, an appearance by the child.

No System of Assessment Is Foolproof

With further testing, SVA or some similar procedure may
offer possibilities for developing a standard system to sift the
relatively small number of false reports from the many true
ones. Psychiatric evaluations can never be foolproof, however,
and the consequences can be "awesome," as Dr. Green notes: "A
mistake might jeopardize a child's future or destroy a man's
family life and career." It's up to the court to make the final
decision, and a judge, on occasion, may be guided by his or her
own intuition.

That happened in an Illinois case. A couple split up after four
years of marriage and agreed to joint custody. A year later, they
were embroiled in a custody battle. The father charged his ex-
wife with sexually abusing their young son and daughter, while
the mother charged her ex-husband with physically abusing
them.

The children were placed in a foster home while a procession
of psychiatrists and social workers questioned them. Seven
months later, the judge awarded custody to the mother, even
though the truth of the charges and countercharges was still up
in the air. "It is apparent to the court that physical, mental and
sexual abuse have taken place . . ." the judge wrote. "But the per-
petrators . . . have not been proven to the satisfaction of the
court."

To Sum Up

Cases involving child abuse and neglect are among the most
difficult and emotional cases a court has to decide. By acting
promptly, getting full medical evidence and competent legal advice, and doing everything you can to reassure and protect the
child, you can help achieve the best possible outcome under the
circumstances.

14

DON'T LET YOUR CHILD BE A VICTIM: PARENTAL KIDNAPPING

In 1967, a divorced father telephoned his ex-wife at the end of a weekend visitation with his 15-month-old daughter and uttered these chilling words: "I'm not bringing the baby home. You'll never see her again." It took more than a year and $10,000 in private investigators' fees for the distraught woman to get her child back. Her ex, as the child's natural father, had broken no kidnapping law. And even though she had a custody order, the state to which her ex had fled didn't recognize it.

Today that story might very likely go much differently. Parental kidnapping laws—unheard of two decades ago—have now been adopted in every state except Tennessee and the District of Columbia to deal with a mounting wave of abductions by noncustodial parents. Virtually every state has made "custodial interference" a felony or a misdemeanor or both. And recent legislation is bringing order into the former chaos of interstate custody disputes.

Still, parental kidnapping goes on, and recovering a child doesn't erase the anguish. In this chapter, I'll not only outline what you can do if your ex kidnaps your child but I'll also suggest ways in which you can prevent that from happening.

What Is Parental Kidnapping, and How Prevalent Is It?

Although definitions vary slightly in different states, parental kidnapping normally occurs when a noncustodial parent (or someone acting for that parent) takes, keeps, or conceals a child from the legal custodian without permission. In some states, the act is considered kidnapping only when a court order has been violated.

People generally think of kidnapping as a cloak-and-dagger-type operation in which a child is spirited away while the parents aren't looking. Parental kidnapping, at the outset, may be less dramatic than that. The noncustodial parent may simply pick up the child at school or keep the child beyond the end of a normal visitation period and refuse to relinquish him or her to the custodial parent. Often, to avoid a court order to return the child, the abductor will take the child to a different state or even to a different country.

A 1981 study estimated approximately one child-snatching for every 22 divorces. Since then, a wave of parental child-stealing has captured media attention. Between June 1984 and January 1988, the National Center for Missing and Exploited Children received approximately 17,500 reports of missing children. (The actual total, including cases not reported to the center, was undoubtedly much larger.) Nearly 6,700—the second largest category after runaways—were victims of parental kidnapping. Fewer than 2,500 of these children have been found, and three have been found dead.

According to a study by two psychologists at the University of Alaska, children who are targets of parental abduction are typically between three and nine years old. The gender of the child apparently makes no difference. Most of the custodial parents who were interviewed felt that the abducting parent was primarily motivated by revenge or by extreme attachment to the child.

If Your Child Is Abducted, Don't Take the Law Into Your Own Hands

Your first impulse, when your child has been abducted, may be to get the child back at all costs. Restrain yourself. If, for example, you break down your ex's door and attempt to grab the child, you may endanger both yourself and your child.

There are a number of legal remedies you can safely pursue—both criminal remedies (prosecution of the offender) and civil remedies (enforcement of custody decrees and filing of damage suits). Keep in mind that every case is different; the overview I'm about to give is no substitute for solid advice from a lawyer who is knowledgeable about your particular case.

Criminal Remedies

In most states, parental kidnapping (sometimes called child abduction, child stealing, custodial interference, or family kidnapping) is a violation of the criminal code. The crime occurs when the abductor knowingly violates an existing custody order.

The custodial parent may be able to press charges against the abductor under the criminal laws either of the child's home state or of the state to which the child was taken. In some states, parental kidnapping is considered a felony, punishable by a jail or prison sentence of more than a year or a heavy fine or both. In other states, it's a misdemeanor, punishable by a shorter sentence or a smaller fine. In some states the offense may be either a felony or a misdemeanor, depending on the circumstances. The Federal Bureau of Investigation can be called in to help catch fugitives in felony cases. In addition to criminal penalties, the abductor, if convicted, may be required to make restitution to the custodial parent for the costs of locating and recovering the child.

Anyone who aids an abductor (for example, by concealing a child) can be charged as an accessory to the crime. In one highly publicized abduction, a father who lost a custody fight nabbed his child and fled to South America. His parents (the child's grandparents) knew where the child had been taken but wouldn't disclose the information. The grandfather was jailed for contempt of court but still refused to talk. Finally the father had to bring the child back to get his father released.

Civil Remedies

Criminal prosecution won't necessarily get your child back. Custody enforcement can be complicated, especially if the abductor has taken the child out of the jurisdiction of the court that issued the original order.

Often the abductor is **forum shopping,** or looking for a state where he or she can get a change of custody. During the past decade or so, state and federal legislation has been adopted to deal with this problem. By 1983, all states had adopted the Uniform Child Custody Jurisdiction Act (UCCJA), which determines whether a state can issue a custody order. The UCCJA has established consistent standards to help state courts decide when they should take jurisdiction over a custody dispute, when to defer to a court in another state, and whether to accept custody decrees from a foreign country.

The federal Parental Kidnapping Prevention Act (PKPA), enacted in 1980, provides that states must honor (that is, enforce and not modify) each other's valid custody orders, giving preference to orders entered in the child's home state. This law, together with the UCCJA, has been effective in discouraging forum shopping.

Another civil remedy available to victims of parental kidnapping is a damage suit. Not only the perpetrator but anyone who helped him or her can be sued for money damages to compensate the victims for their suffering.

Locating the Abductor and Your Child

Before you can prosecute, sue, or enforce a custody order, the first step is to search for the abductor and your child. Several resources are available to help.

The computerized Federal Parent Locator Service, originally

set up to track down child support dodgers, can be used to trace parental kidnappers through their Social Security numbers. Also, the FBI can enter descriptions of missing children into its National Crime Information Center (NCIC) computer, whether or not an abductor is charged with a crime.

The National Center for Missing and Exploited Children, a resource center created by federal law, operates a toll-free hotline (see Box 8) for parents to report a missing child. Anyone who has information that could lead to the recovery of a child can use the hotline. Many states have established clearinghouses to help parents find and recover missing children, and a network of nonprofit agencies also exists to help. In addition, state laws provide for special registries and identification programs in the schools.

Preventing Child Abduction

Here's a common scenario for child abduction. The noncustodial parent goes to the child's school and tells the teacher that something has come up and the child needs to be dismissed early. The teacher, knowing nothing of the custody arrangement, complies. The abducting parent thus has several hours of lead time before the child is expected home—time during which the custodial parent won't be aware of the kidnapping and thus won't alert authorities.

In many of these cases, the abduction could have been prevented. According to the superintendent of an affluent school district on Chicago's suburban North Shore, many parents—in a misguided effort to keep a separation or divorce quiet—fail to inform the school of a child's custodial status. If the custodial parent took the precaution of notifying school authorities, they would know to whom they should or should not release the child. The school should be given a certified copy of the custody order and should be instructed to alert the custodial parent of any unscheduled visits by the noncustodial parent. The same goes for day care centers and babysitters.

Of course, if there's no custody order, either parent has a perfect right to take physical possession of the child or to give someone else permission to do it. Therefore it's very important for the

Box 8

What To Do If Your Child Has Been Abducted

•File a missing person report with your local police department.

•Ask local or state authorities to request the FBI to enter your child's description in the computerized list at the National Crime Information Center (NCIC).

•Call the National Center for Missing and Exploited Children (NCMEC) toll-free hotline (1-800-843-5678) to report your child missing.

•Actively participate in the search for your child. Contact organizations that may be able to help. NCMEC can furnish a list.

•Meet with your local prosecuting attorney and decide whether to press criminal charges against the abductor. If the abductor is to be charged with a felony, make sure the warrant is entered into the NCIC computer. If the abductor has fled the state, ask the prosecutor to get a federal warrant so the FBI can be called in to assist in the search.

•If you don't already have legal custody, obtain a temporary custody order immediately. If you already have custody, get extra certified or notarized copies of your decree from the clerk of the court that issued it. When your child is located, you should promptly send a copy of your custody order to the family court in that jurisdiction.

•Ask the police to help you get your child back when the abductor is apprehended. In most states, the police are not

obliged to return the child to you; you may need to petition the family court where the child is located to enforce
your custody decree. If you fear that the abductor will flee
with the child when notified of the enforcement proceeding, you can ask the court for a pickup order, which directs
enforcement officers to pick up the child.

•After your child is returned to you, ask the court that issued your custody decree to restrict visitation or to order
supervised visitation and to add other safeguards (such as
posting a bond) to prevent another abduction.

•Be prepared to seek psychological counseling for yourself
and your child to deal with the emotional aftereffects of the
experience. Remember that, despite your own feelings,
your child may still want and need to carry on a relationship with the other parent.

For More Information and Help

•The National Center for Missing and Exploited Children,
1835 K Street, N.W., Suite 600, Washington, D.C. 20006, in
cooperation with the American Bar Association and the
U.S. Department of Justice, has prepared a comprehensive
handbook, *Parental Kidnapping: How to Prevent an Abduction and What to Do If Your Child Is Abducted.* The list of action steps above, as well as some of the other material in
this chapter, is adapted from the revised edition published
in August 1988. In addition to operating its missing
children hotline, the center has a staff of attorneys with expertise in parental kidnapping, who can answer questions
and provide guidance to lawyers and law enforcement officials.

person raising and caring for a child after a divorce or separation to get a custody order. A national survey of police departments found that one of the greatest obstacles to successful investigation of parental kidnappings is difficulty in verifying who has custody.

Certain safeguards can be written into the custody order; if they aren't already there, the decree can be modified to include them. For example, specific visitation schedules are safer than a vague provision for reasonable visitation, which has no clear-cut endpoint. The decree can also limit the right of the noncustodial parent to take the child out of state or even out of town. (Such a provision is especially wise if the noncustodial parent has an occupation that affords mobility, or if he or she has family ties in another place.)

Many child abductions could be avoided if the custodial parent took the other parent's threats seriously. Potential child-snatchers often tip their hands in advance. The University of Alaska study I mentioned earlier found that in 60 percent of parental kidnappings, the act had been preceded by threats or unsuccessful attempts. (Only 9 percent of divorced parents in a control group that had not experienced abductions had received such threats.)

If your ex threatens to abduct your child, you might ask the police or prosecutor to talk to him or her about the possible criminal consequences of such an act. If you have evidence of the intended abduction, you can ask a court to force the other parent to post bond to guarantee the child's return after visitation. Be alert to any signs of preparations for a move, such as selling a house, quitting a job, or closing a bank account.

International Abductions

The problem of child abductions across international lines was highlighted in May 1988 when United Press International reported that Peter O'Toole, who had taken his five-year-old son, Lorcan, to London, was defying a New Jersey court order to turn over the boy to his mother. According to the UPI release, the Irish-born actor, who had never married the mother, was supposed to return Lorcan to her in April under terms of a joint custody agreement worked out two months before. When he didn't, the New Jersey court ordered the boy's return. But O'Toole refused, claiming he was acting in the best interest of the child. The mother's lawyer reportedly planned to seek an arrest warrant for O'Toole. But the actor, who was in London, couldn't be arrested unless he returned to the United States.

Getting back a child who has been taken to another state is hard enough; getting back a child who has been taken to another country can be almost hopeless. And the problem has grown. Five years ago, the State Department knew of 667 unsolved cases of child abductions from this country. In 1987, the caseload topped 2,300, and 300 new cases were coming in each year.

When a child is abducted and taken abroad, the other parent must first locate the child—a task that generally requires a private detective. Once the child has been found, if the abductor refuses to return the child, the other parent faces a long uphill battle in foreign courts.

To cut through the red tape, the United States and several other nations (including, so far, Canada, France, Portugal, Spain, Switzerland, Hungary, the United Kingdom, Luxembourg, and Australia) have approved a treaty called the Hague Convention on the Civil Aspects of International Child Abduction. The treaty was negotiated in 1980 and went into effect in the U.S. on July 1, 1988 after Congress adopted implementing legislation.

Under the Hague Convention, with very limited exceptions, abducted children who are taken to a signatory nation must be returned home for a custody determination by a local court unless a judge finds a danger to the child in doing so. This provision applies even if there's no previous custody order. Thus the fate of an American child in most cases will no longer be determined by a foreign court—if the country to which the child has been taken has signed the treaty.

The hope is that the treaty will deter parents from wrongfully removing or retaining children abroad. The treaty also facilitates exercise of visitation rights across international borders.

Each country that ratifies the Hague Convention must set up a Central Authority to implement it. In the U.S., the Central

Authority is the Office of Citizens Consular Services of the State Department. If you believe your child has been abducted to a foreign country, you should contact this office to find out what to do. The Central Authority can tap into the domestic Parent Locator Service.

The Hague Convention applies only to cases that arise after ratification. Parents whose children were abducted before July 1, 1988 or were taken to countries that have not yet ratified the convention will not be able to take advantage of it.

A case I handled illustrates what can happen in the absence of such a treaty. In this case, I represented a father whose ex-wife had custody of their three children. She remarried, and her new husband got a job in Colombia. When she petitioned for permission to move the children there, we objected and the court said no. Thumbing her nose at the court, she did it anyway.

My client had a court order forbidding his ex to take the children out of the country. But as far as the Colombian courts were concerned, the order wasn't worth the paper it was printed on. After trying fruitlessly to get the order enforced via long distance, my client finally hopped a plane, determined to get those kids himself. What happened? You guessed it. The Colombian police arrested him for child-snatching and gave him a choice between jail and deportation. He chose the latter, and he hasn't seen his children in three years.

If you're dealing with a country that hasn't ratified the Hague Convention, there are a number of things you can try, short of getting yourself in trouble with foreign police. In searching for your child, you can seek help from INTERPOL, an international police agency, from the U.S. Customs Service, and from the U.S. State Department. You can ask your local prosecutor to get a federal warrant for unlawful flight to avoid prosecution and then ask the U.S. passport office to revoke the abductor's passport. You can pursue international extradition. If the abductor is a foreign national, you can alert U.S. immigration authorities to intercept him or her upon any attempt to reenter this country. You can file suit in the courts of the country to which your child was taken. Be aware, though, that the process is likely to be long and complicated, and your chances of recovering your child may be slim.

Preventing an International Abduction

What steps can a custodial parent take if there's reason to believe that the noncustodial parent intends to take a child out of the country? First, check your custody order. Does it specifically prohibit such removal? If not, and if you believe that your ex may try it, you can seek a modification to put such a provision in the decree. While you're at it, you can ask the court to require your ex to post bond to ensure that the child isn't taken out of the country, or that, if taken out for a lawful visit, the child will be returned.

If one parent is a citizen of a foreign country, the other parent should be especially alert to the possibility of an international abduction. Joint custody can be particularly dangerous in families with mixed citizenship. But even with sole custody, the danger is there. The foreign parent may feel that it's important for the child to be raised according to the values of that parent's culture.

In one case, a registered nurse in Cicero, Illinois, married a student from Saudi Arabia. The couple had two little girls and then divorced. The mother was awarded custody, but the father took the children to Saudi Arabia and refused to return them. Because Saudi Arabia hadn't signed the Hague Convention, the mother had no standing in the courts of that country to get her daughters back.

One precaution that can be taken to prevent such a situation is to ask a court, before allowing any foreign travel with the child, to order the foreign parent to obtain a pronouncement from the government or courts of his or her country, recognizing the validity of the custody order and the continuing exclusive jurisdiction of U.S. courts.

Another wise precaution is to make sure no passport can be issued for the child. I had a case in which a divorced father threatened to take his two-year-old son to the father's native Greece. The mother, who had sole custody, took the threat seriously. I obtained an injunction on her behalf, prohibiting removal of the child from the jurisdiction of the court. We registered the injunction, along with her custody order, with immigration authorities. The threatened abduction never took place.

Is There Ever A Good Reason for Child-Snatching?

Most of the time, parental kidnapping doesn't occur out of the blue. Generally it's the climax to an escalating sequence of disputes over child support, visitation, and other issues. In some cases, it's the product of a disturbed or vindictive mind. But often it's a result of frustration and desperation on the part of a noncustodial parent who feels that there's no other way to preserve his or her relationship with the child.

Some abductors honestly feel that they are doing the best thing for their children by removing them from the influence of the custodial parent. But regardless of the motive, children are bound to suffer when torn from their homes, separated from one parent, and forced into a fugitive existence.

It's important for prospective abductors to realize that there are legal means of dealing with their concerns. If the custodial parent is denying or interfering with visitation, there are remedies. If the custodial parent threatens to remove the child from the state, it's possible to oppose and block such a move. If the custodial parent is a bad influence on the child, it should be possible to get a change of custody.

When there's evidence that a child is being abused or neglected, it may be essential to act quickly to remove the child. If possible, custody should be obtained before taking the child. The UCCJA gives courts the power to take emergency jurisdiction and order temporary custody. Once the order has been entered, the person who has obtained custody can't be charged with kidnapping.

If you feel it's too dangerous to wait to remove the child, you may be able to petition for emergency relief afterward. While I don't recommend such action as a general rule, there are rare occasions when taking the law into your own hands is the only way to protect a child.

A young single woman had an affair with a married man and gave the baby to him and his wife to raise, but they never got a custody order. When the little girl was five years old, the mother (who, up to that point, had shown no interest in her) married and moved to New York. She asked the father if she could take the child there for two weeks to meet her new husband's family, and the father agreed. But at the end of that time, the mother refused to return the little girl or even to let him talk to her on the phone. When he flew to New York, the mother refused to let him see the child.

The father, feeling that something was very wrong, called the police, who did a cursory check and then dropped the matter. Finally the desperate father took drastic action. He found out where the child was going to kindergarten, picked her up there (she went willingly and quietly), and flew home with her. On the plane, the little girl confided that her stepfather had been touching her private parts, and that her mother had told her it was all right "because he's your new Daddy; he can touch you wherever he wants."

The father took his daughter straight from the airport to a hospital emergency room, where the doctors found bruising and swelling in the vaginal area. He immediately contacted me, and we filed for and secured temporary custody on an emergency basis.

Of course, the father took a calculated risk when he spirited the child away without a custody order. The mother called the police and the FBI. But because we moved so quickly for emergency custody, and because the law enforcement officers believed the child's story, and because the Illinois criminal code provides for a short grace period in cases of abuse or neglect, my client escaped arrest.

Remember, though, these emergency provisions are intended only for exceptional, urgent cases. If you're thinking of snatching your child or grandchild, you must realize that you may be in for trouble unless you can convince a court that your action was justified under the circumstances.

PART V

Keeping Up With the Law

15

KEEP YOUR EYE ON THE TAX CODE

One of the exciting aspects of family law is that it's constantly changing and evolving. New legislation and new trends in court decisions constantly offer new challenges and opportunities to a practitioner on the lookout for creative ways to protect and advance a client's interests.

In these last two chapters, I'll touch briefly on two important areas in which statutory and case law is changing. In this chapter, I'll give you a brief overview of tax law revisions affecting divorced and separated persons; to find out how these changes may apply specifically to your situation, you should, of course, see your own attorney and/or accountant. In the final chapter, I'll discuss the emerging trend toward suits for sexual liability.

Can New Laws Affect Old Decrees?

How do recent tax reforms affect the deal you thought you had with your ex? Normally a change in the tax laws doesn't apply to you if your decree, order, or agreement predates the change. As a general rule, you're stuck with, or safe with, whatever the law was at the time your instrument was executed. But that's not always true.

Since 1984, Congress has overhauled the rules of the game for divorce taxation. A few of these changes may have an impact on existing arrangements. And many of the new rules can be made to apply to preexisting decrees if the parties want them to. In other words, in many instances you can opt to come under the new law rather than the old. Expert advice is crucial to determine whether it would be advantageous to incorporate a particular change into your decree, and whether any adverse effects might result.

Transferring Property Tax-free

The 1984 Domestic Relations Tax Reform Act (part of the Deficit Reduction Act of that year) changed the tax effects of a property transfer between spouses. The change also applies to a transfer between ex-spouses if the transfer is "incident to a divorce."

Under a 1962 U.S. Supreme Court decision that came to be known as the **Davis rule**, if the man, for example, under the terms of a divorce settlement, signed over title of the family home to the woman, the transfer was considered equivalent to a sale. Thus, if the home had appreciated in value, the man was required to pay tax on the capital gain even though he was giving the property to the woman.

Under the 1984 act, such a transfer is now treated as a gift. The man doesn't have to report a capital gain (nor, if the property has depreciated, can he report a capital loss). Regardless of the value of the house at the time of the transfer, if the woman later sells it, she'll figure her capital gain or loss on the basis of the original value when it was purchased, plus the value of any improvements.

You may be able to take advantage of this new provision—which also applies to annuities, life insurance, and other transfers—even if you're already divorced. The change may apply, if both parties agree, to transfers made after the 1984 tax law was enacted, if the transfer is pursuant to the provisions of an older decree. Normally the transfer must occur within six years after the divorce. Thus, if your decree, issued in 1983, called for your ex to transfer the house to you in 1989, the two of you can jointly elect to have the transfer treated as a gift not subject to capital gains tax.

Obviously, this would be a windfall for your ex. But you may be able to turn it to your advantage as well, through some creative bargaining. Since the capital gains tax was undoubtedly taken into consideration in the negotiation of your property settlement, you may be able to get your ex to agree that in return for your going along with treating the transfer as a gift, it's fair to make some other modification in your favor—say, an increase in alimony—to balance the scales.

Be aware, though, that if you and your ex choose to treat the transfer of the house as a gift, you must do the same for any other property transfers made under your decree.

Changing the Rules for Alimony

The alimony section of the 1984 act contains several important changes that may apply to a pre-1985 decree if the decree is modified to say so. (The new rules also apply to a post-1985 decree that replaces an earlier separation agreement if the alimony provisions of the decree differ from those of the earlier agreement.) Some of the new rules may be to your advantage; others may not. You and your tax advisor need to weigh the pros and cons before you decide whether to seek to modify your decree to come under the new law.

For example, alimony payments, which are deductible by the payor and taxable to the payee, no longer need be periodic; even a single cash payment may qualify. However, the 1984 act also introduced complicated rules that limit the deductibility of large maintenance payments made within the first few years following a divorce or separation (front-loaded payments). A 1986 amendment somewhat loosened these 1984 front-loading restrictions.

The 1986 amendment increases from $10,000 to $15,000 the amount a payor can deduct in a given year without risk of losing the deduction; it also reduces from six to three the number of consecutive post-separation years during which deductions for payments in excess of that amount may be disallowed (under a statutory formula). These changes can be made to apply to a pre-1987 decree by modification. If not, a decree executed in 1985 or 1986 will still come under the 1984 rules, as will an older decree that's modified to incorporate those rules.

Allocating Unallocated Support

The 1984 tax law sought to close a loophole created by the Supreme Court's long-standing ruling in the case of *Commissioner v. Lester* regarding unallocated support payments. Under the **Lester rule**, all such payments, which combine alimony and child support, were treated as alimony. This was important because the tax treatment of child support is the opposite of the treatment of alimony: child support is tax-free to the recipient, and the payor can't deduct it. Since alimony is deductible by the payor, a man could avoid paying taxes on money he contributed for child support if his divorce agreement lumped this sum with alimony and called it unallocated support.

There's no such thing as "unallocated support" under the new tax laws. Payments to an ex-spouse are now supposed to be separated into alimony and child support. Congress provided a way of tripping up evaders of this rule: amounts designated as alimony will instead be treated as child support for tax purposes if they hinge on an event related to a child, such as the child's marriage or attainment of a certain age. If, for example, the decree provides that maintenance will be cut in half upon the child's reaching age 18, the payor will be able to deduct only half of the total, and the recipient will include only half in taxable income. Again, however, this change doesn't apply to a pre-1985 decree unless it's modified to incorporate the 1984 reforms.

The elimination of unallocated support means that it now takes much more creative draftsmanship to achieve the optimal balance between alimony and child support in a divorce settlement. Before the 1984 tax bracket reductions, unallocated support was often a very good deal for both parties. If a man was in a high tax bracket, the deduction enabled him to pay the woman more than he otherwise might have been willing or able to do.

For example, if he was in the 50 percent bracket, he could give the woman $12,000 at a true cost to him of only $6,000. She, in turn, got $6,000 more than the man would otherwise have agreed to, and—if she was in the lowest tax bracket—she probably paid no more than $2,000 of it in taxes.

Now there's no more 50 percent tax bracket, and if the man is in the 28 or 33 percent bracket, the deal may not seem as good to him as it originally did. Can he then modify the amount of maintenance? Maybe or maybe not. If I was representing this man, I might argue that in addition to his not getting as much of a tax break as the agreement contemplated, the higher cost of living is cutting into his available income. If, in addition, the woman's earning capacity has increased, the combination of factors might convince a court to modify, even though the tax change alone might not.

Who Gets the Dependency Exemption?

The 1984 law changed the rules that determine which parent can claim a child as a dependent. Before, either parent could claim the exemption, depending on the amount each contributed for support and on whether the parties, in their decree or agreement, had specified which parent could claim it. The new act presumes that the custodial parent is providing more than half of the child's support and gives that parent the exemption, unless he or she waives it in writing. The waiver, which the noncustodial parent must attach to his or her tax return, can apply to a single year, a number of specified years (such as alternate years), or all future years. (However, a custodial parent who waives the exemption would be well advised to make the declaration on an annual basis rather than for a longer period, so as to retain leverage to ensure the receipt of child support payments.)

If you're the custodial parent, can you now take the exemption even though your decree or agreement gave it to your ex? No. If you refuse to sign the waiver, you can be held in contempt of court for failing to live up to the terms of the order. (Of course, if your decree doesn't say anything about who gets the exemption, you get it unless you choose to waive it.) If you're the noncustodial parent and your decree or agreement entitles you to the exemption, you must make sure that your ex signs the waiver.

There's one other wrinkle, which applies to decrees that were in force before this reform was adopted. If your decree was executed before 1985 and states that your ex-husband is entitled to the exemption, he can continue to take it, even without your signing the waiver, as long as he chips in at least $600 a year for the child's support—unless the decree is modified to say that this provision won't apply. If you as the custodial parent are contributing most of the child's support, yet your ex is still kicking in that $600 and getting the exemption, you might consider filing a petition to modify the decree. You might argue that changed circumstances (such as your ex's failure to provide the full amount of support he was ordered to make) justify the modification, consistent with the intent of the 1984 tax amendments.

Medical expenses are an exception to the new dependency rules. Either parent can deduct hospital or doctor bills that he or she pays for a child, even if the other parent claims the dependency exemption. However, only the custodial parent is entitled to the credit for child-care expenses.

To Sum Up

If you've managed to read through this whole chapter, you may feel hopelessly confused. Don't worry—you're not alone. Even tax experts are unsure about some of the ramifications of the reforms. These provisions are quite new, and until the Supreme Court rules on a particular question, different revenue agents and different courts may interpret it differently.

My main purpose in this chapter has been to demonstrate the importance of keeping your eye on the tax code. Again, I must emphasize that you should get professional advice about the impact of current or future tax reforms on your particular situation.

16

SEXUAL LIABILITY: A NEW ROAD TO COURT

A Minneapolis woman who claimed that a sex partner had infected her with herpes collected $25,000 from his homeowners' insurance, which covered claims for bodily injury, sickness, or disease.

A father is suing to get out of paying child support because when the child was conceived the mother told him she was using birth control.

A woman who became infertile as a result of a tubal pregnancy is suing the man who assured her that there was no way he could get her pregnant.

These are but a few of the recent developments in the burgeoning field of sexual liability law. Not only former lovers but estranged mates and ex-spouses are beginning to sue partners they claim gave them sexually transmitted diseases, unwanted pregnancies, or other troubles.

In addition, the old-fashioned breach-of-promise or alienation-of-affections suit is making a comeback despite traditional concerns about privacy, perjury, and difficulty of proof. Creative lawyers are finding loopholes in state laws that have barred suits by former lovers seeking to trade hard feelings for hard cash. Such suits are becoming increasingly popular with jilted women who have no recourse in the divorce courts but who are saying, "I'm mad as hell and I'm not going to take it any more."

Breaking the Marital Shield

Another expression of the trend toward accountability is the breakdown of what's called **interspousal tort immunity**, which historically shielded husbands and wives from damage suits for wrongful actions committed against each other. One rationale for these immunity laws, which also banned suits by ex-spouses for injuries inflicted during the marriage, was to shield the courts from a barrage of nuisance suits—domestic spats elevated to courtroom capers.

As early as 1962, 18 states had abolished interspousal tort immunity. A California Supreme Court ruling that year allowed a negligence suit by a wife who had slipped and fallen on the deck of her husband's boat. The dissent in the case forecast that it would bring on a flood of spiteful or petty litigation. But it's doubtful that anyone then foresaw a spate of suits reaching into the most intimate recesses of the heart and the bedroom.

As more and more states end interspousal tort immunity (as Illinois did in 1988), virtually any claim of intentional injury or negligence—careless or reckless conduct that may have contributed to an injury—may become a legitimate cause of action. The Missouri Supreme Court in 1986 permitted a woman whose divorce was about to be granted to sue her estranged husband for shooting her in the back. The Texas Supreme Court the following year let a woman sue her husband for negligence for injuries she received while riding his motorcycle. If a married or formerly married woman can sue for being shot or shaken up, why not for being impregnated against her will or infected without her knowledge?

It's increasingly being recognized that married women can be raped, that they can be abused—physically and mentally—and that they are entitled to redress. (In 1984, New York became the seventeenth state to abolish the traditional exemption of marital rape from criminal prosecution. However, as of 1987, the exemption still existed in at least 9 states, and in 26 others it was lifted only under specific circumstances, such as a legal separation.)

A Houston jury early in 1988 awarded a woman, in addition to her divorce settlement, $500,000 in damages for mental cruelty inflicted by the philandering of her millionaire husband. The Missouri Supreme Court in 1986 allowed a woman to charge her husband with negligence for giving her a venereal disease.

Such recourse may make economic sense, especially in these days of easy divorce. Suppose a couple are married only six months, and within that time, the well-to-do husband manages to give his wife a severe case of herpes. In terms of the usual elements of a settlement, there may be nothing much to the divorce case: short marriage, no children, no jointly-purchased property. She most likely has a job and isn't a candidate for alimony. Yet simple justice seems to dictate that she should have some kind of cause of action against this man.

In one such case I'm handling, my client is suing her ex-husband for intentional infliction of emotional distress during their brief marriage. The man, who is considerably older than the woman and had been married before, wanted no more children. When she became pregnant, he gave her an ultimatum: if she wanted to stay married to him, she must have an abortion. After much agonizing, she did. When she became pregnant again, he insisted that she have a tubal ligation or else he'd leave her. Again she gave in. A few months later, he took up with another woman and served his wife with divorce papers.

This case, like many of those that have come up so far, was initially filed while the couple were still married but in the throes of divorce. As the trend builds, we can expect to see more such suits filed by ex-wives—and ex-husbands, too—for wrongs committed during a marriage.

Since this area of the law is just now being explored, there's no way of knowing how many of these suits will be entertained by the courts or, if heard, will succeed. Can a noncustodial parent whose visitation rights have been interfered with sue the custodial parent for emotional distress? A Wisconsin court said no, but perhaps another court would say yes. Remember, too, in some states interspousal tort immunity still exists.

Another Bite at the Apple?

In addition, there are questions to be ironed out about the connection, if any, between divorce cases and later damage suits between the same parties. A New Hampshire court, in 1987, held that a divorce decree didn't prevent a later tort suit because that kind of lawsuit is fundamentally different from a divorce. In a Wisconsin case the same year, an ex-wife was allowed to file a tort suit against her ex-husband after she had obtained a no-fault divorce. But in a 1987 Tennessee case, the Appellate Court refused to permit a tort action after a divorce on grounds that the issue had been dealt with in the divorce case itself and couldn't be brought up again. This principle is called **res judicata**, which, loosely translated, means "The issue has been decided."

What res judicata means, in this context, is that you can't use a tort suit as an excuse to retry your divorce case. For example, suppose a woman, during a divorce proceeding, claims that her husband abused her. He denies it, and the divorce court finds no basis for the charge. If, after the divorce, the woman tries to file a damage suit for abuse that allegedly occurred during the marriage, the court may say, "Look, you already brought up those same charges in your divorce case, and the judge said you didn't have any basis for them." (On the other hand, she'd most likely be allowed to raise new charges of abuse based on events occurring after the divorce.)

It's not difficult to imagine a different scenario in which a court might hold that a tort suit after a divorce was not res judicata. Suppose a man has an alcohol problem. He and his wife get into an argument over his drinking at a party. He insists on driving home and gets into an accident. She's thrown into the windshield and spends weeks in the hospital. The incident is the last straw, as far as she's concerned, and she files for divorce. Since her state has a no-fault statute, and marital misconduct isn't a factor in determining property division there, the man's drinking and driving don't enter into the suit. So, if she later makes a claim for damages for the injuries she sustained in the crash, a court may well view the issue as a fresh one that wasn't litigated in connection with the divorce.

Where Is All This Leading?

The cases reported so far have provoked imaginative speculations. Some journalists and lawyers have envisioned fascinating new questions for dispute, some serious and some trivial. If a man gets drunk and abuses his wife, can she sue? What if he claims that her frigidity made him impotent? What if he tells her he had a vasectomy, but she conceives and then suffers a miscarriage? What if he gives her AIDS? What if she has an affair with his boss and destroys his career? On a more mundane note, what if she won't get up early to make his breakfast? What if she thinks he gambles too much? The possibilities are endless. According to some soothsayers, husbands and wives will have to tiptoe through marriage, worrying that anything they say or do may later be held against them.

Some of this fantasizing may be largely sensationalism. For one thing, practically speaking, there's a financial constraint. Litigation costs money. A suit isn't likely to be filed unless the defendant has substantial assets or insurance. And, by and large, insurance companies aren't going to be willing to foot the bill for marital misbehavior (even though they may have no similar out with regard to unwed relationships).

Intentional wrongs, like punching someone in the nose, generally aren't insurable regardless of any marital relationship; public policy dictates against this. So, if you want to collect from your ex's insurance, you'll probably have to show that he or she was reckless or careless. But first you'd better check the policy. After the Texas motorcycle case, the State Board of Insurance authorized an endorsement for automobile policies excluding liability coverage for damage suits between family members. In Illinois, among other states, such an exemption has been standard on automobile and homeowners' policies for a long time.

These exemptions are bound to have a chilling effect on interspousal tort suits. It's one thing to sue an insurance company for a million dollars; it's another thing to sue your mate or your ex directly, knowing it's unlikely that you can collect.

Another point to consider: there's generally a two- or three-year statute of limitations on this type of action. So it might seem that a case involving ex-spouses would have to be filed fairly soon after the divorce. But these statutes normally begin running only when the injury is discovered. So, for example, if it takes six years for a woman to find out she has AIDS, it may still be possible for her to get a damage award against her ex if she can show that he was the source.

In a developing area of the law like this one, it's especially important not to jump to conclusions but to see a knowledgeable lawyer who can advise you about your particular case.

A Last Word: Is Accountability Coming Back?

It's impossible to predict with certainty how far a trend will go. Today's legal quirk may become tomorrow's axiom. Fifteen years ago, there were no laws on grandparents' visitation rights; today these rights, in some form, are almost universally accepted.

What I believe we're seeing today is the beginning of a tremendous ground swell of feeling and opinion against the oversimplification of divorce and cohabitation. It may well be that the wave of no-accountability epitomized by no-fault divorce has peaked.

During the 1960s and 1970s, love, sex, marriage, and divorce became free and easy. Couples said, "Let's give it a try, and if it doesn't work out, no harm done, no hard feelings. If we decide to get married, we can always divorce and split everything 50-50. Hey, it's been fun! You go your way, I'll go mine. Why should some judge tell us how we should live our lives?"

Now, many people are saying, "Wait a minute, it's not so simple. Men and women are being hurt, children are involved. You can't just say *adios* and that's the end of it."

As our society becomes increasingly litigious, more and more people are realizing that sex isn't necessarily free, and a person can't just drift in and out of someone else's life leaving a deposit of pain without penalty. As long as men and women are human,